CONTENTS

HOW TO BECOME A MILLIONAIRE IN 5, 10, OR 15, YEARS...

Introduction 3

1. Planning for Retirement 5

2. Early Retirement Goals 22

3. Rental Property Primer 41

4. Build Your Real Estate Team 63

5. Finding the Right Property 80

6. Getting a Good Deal 90

7. Maintaining Your Investments 113

8. Real Estate Investing Mistakes to Avoid 129

Conclusion 139

HOW TO TURN YOUR SIDE HUSTLE INTO A PASSIVE INCOME SOURCE

Introduction 143

1. What Is Passive Income? 145

2. How to Choose a Source of Passive Income 153

3. Passive Income Ideas- Online 159

4. Passive Income Ideas- In Person 205

5. Passive Income Ideas- Skill Requiring 222

6. Financial Information 238

7. How To Make This A Reality 257

Afterword 263

HOW TO BECOME A
MILLIONAIRE
IN 5, 10, OR 15, YEARS...

Your Road Map to Financial Freedom

NATHIN O'BRIEN

INTRODUCTION

The goal of the book is to teach people how they will be able to retire comfortably through the ultimate use of real estate investment, but some ancillary topics are covered as well.

Let's be honest here – we all wish for a retirement where we can pursue our hobbies or sip that perfect cocktail on some posh island somewhere in the Bahamas. I do, don't you? But in order to turn that dream into a reality, you have to start somewhere. Early retirement is gaining popularity every day, and here, in this book, we are going to discuss whether it is really possible to retire early and also have all the good things in life.

Let me give you a brief answer to your question – yes, it's possible, and if you ask how? It's through real estate investment. Don't worry – I know some of you may be thinking that it's not your cup of tea but hear me out – no one is born knowing everything. Everything that you know today, you have learned at some point in your life. Real estate investing is nothing different. All you need to do is start learning, and with proper planning, you will have set up everything in no time.

So, what are you waiting for? Go ahead and take your first step towards a better future.

PLANNING FOR RETIREMENT

NO MATTER YOUR AGE, it is never too soon to start planning a budget for retirement. While this may seem premature or simply too much trouble at the current time, the fact of the matter is that the sooner you have a plan in place, the sooner you can stop stressing about it and the more fun you will be able to have once the big day arrives. What's more, the sooner you plan out how you would like your retirement to look, the sooner you can start making investments that will help you get to where you need to be.

There are numerous different factors that are going to affect your retirement, including savings, inflation, spending, part-time earnings, social security, pensions, taxes, retirement date, and, of course, investments and their rates of return. With so many factors in play, it is important to have a general idea of a budget in mind to ensure you will be able to have the right type of lifestyle once you do finally get to retire. You've worked hard all of your life to provide for yourself and your family;

retirement should be a reward, not a burden, and having a budget in place will ensure this is the case.

CREATING A RETIREMENT BUDGET

In order to create a retirement plan that is right for you, the first thing you are going to need to do is to determine where you are currently at and what your monthly retirement budget is going to be. This means you are going to need the past year's worth of bank account statements and credit card statements, as well as the last two paystubs you and your partner (if you are married) received. Having your last tax return on hand is also recommended. This will help you to determine where your money has been going, so you can determine where it is likely to go in the future. With everything laid out in front of you, you will then want to group expenses into the following categories.

Fixed Expenses

Your current budget should start with a list of all of your annual, quarterly, and monthly payments; this list should further be broken down into three main categories. Essentials are things like health care, transportation, housing, clothing, and food. Non-essential obligations are things like subscriptions, gym memberships, cable, and anything else that you could cut out of your budget if the need arises. Finally, you will want to group together essential expenses that are less frequent such as property taxes, home warranties, auto registration, and insurance premiums. For these non-monthly expenses, you will want to break down the monthly costs for ease of use.

．　．　．

*W*ith all of your expenses broken down, you will then want to make a spreadsheet to easily account for all of the data. You will want all of the months listed across the horizontal access and all of the expenses listed on the vertical access. You will want to come up with a firm total that you spend each month.

*T*ake Increasing Health Care Costs Into Account

It doesn't matter if your employer has been paying the bill for your health care costs or if you work for yourself; as you age, your health care costs are going to increase. In fact, on average, premiums for those between the ages of 60 and 65 tend to run about $1,000 per month per person. During this step, you are going to want to look into insurance plans that fit your anticipated needs so that you can have at least a reasonable estimate about what to expect.

*D*on't forget to include costs for hearing, eye care, and dental, as leaving anything out now will create a hole in your plan that won't be as easy to fill later on. It is important to estimate these costs as accurately as possible, as being off by just a little bit can easily throw your entire plan out of whack.

*O*ptional Expenses

With the requirements out of the way, it will then be time to consider all of the fun things you are going to want to do for your retirement. Consider the hobbies that you have now and those that you will have time for once you no longer need to be concerned about working. Consider if you want to travel and where you will want to go as well as how frequently you will want to go there. As you will be working from a fixed income at that point, it is important to consider potential compromises you would be willing to make to support your hobbies in the long term. For example, if you want to spend your retirement traveling, you may want to consider downsizing your domicile; after all, you probably no longer have the space requirements that you once did, and if you are traveling all the time, you likely won't be home much anyway.

Consider Flex Versus Fixed Expenses

Once you have tallied up all of your expenses, you will want to total up all of those that are non-negotiable first. You will then want to subtract that number from your total expenses to determine what your fixed requirements are and what your flexible requirements are. If you like what you see, then great! Otherwise, you will need to take a harder look at both and determine where changes can be made to get things into alignment. For example, if you still have a hefty mortgage and car payments, then you may want to consider ways to get those out of the way before you retire. A good rule of thumb is that if you hope to have more fun after you retire, you will want to lower your fixed expenses as much as possible to free up funds for flexible spending later on.

EXPENSES TO WATCH OUT FOR

Even after you have created a basic plan, it can be easy for certain expenses to creep up on you without notice. The following list has things that many future retirees don't consider when planning their budgets.

. . .

True Costs of a New Hobby

While you may have been dreaming about taking up that special hobby for years, the fact of the matter is that it likely costs more than you think to really get into it in a big way. Expensive hobbies are one of the easiest ways to drain your retirement coffers faster than you would like. In fact, nearly 60 percent of recent retirees tend to overspend in their first five years of retirement, simply because there is so much more to do out there than they originally anticipated.

Home Renovations

Unless you are a contractor or something similar, it can be very difficult to accurately determine the costs associated with even the simplest round of home renovations. These renovations don't even need to be purely cosmetic, and a commonly overlooked cost is that associated with replacing a roof, something that many older homes are going to need to be done at least once in your lifetime. If you can't take care of these costs prior to retirement, it is best to set aside a chunk of funds as an emergency reserve for them down the line, just in case.

Children

Especially these days, just because your children are grown doesn't mean that you won't find yourself in a situation where they are going to ask you for financial help. If you feel as though you are going to be inclined to lend a helping hand when asked, it is important to ensure that you have the money on hand to give what is asked without it negatively affecting you in the future. If you have a child or two who is prone to these types of requests, then set aside a little extra for this inevitability.

*L*ikewise, if you have a child with special needs who will continue to rely on you after you reach retirement, then it is important to factor their needs into your plan as well. When doing so, it is important to keep in mind that after a child with special needs turns 18, their social security restrictions are no longer tied to your own, and any adult who is diagnosed with special needs prior to turning 22 is eligible for social security disability insurance benefits based on your social security earnings. However, this can be a double-edged sword as if you ensure your child is too well taken care of, then this can disqualify them from certain benefits, so it is important to work with a knowledgeable attorney to determine what is right for your child.

*P*arental Care

If you expect to have to care for an elderly parent after your retirement, it is important to factor in these costs as well. The potential costs for such an endeavor can vary wildly based on the parent's health and expectations, so it is important to have a frank conversation with them about their own retirement funds and what they see as their plan for the future. You only have so much time to plan for your own retirement, and it is important to have concrete financial plans in place while you can still do things to change your financial plan.

POTENTIAL RETIREMENT INVESTMENTS

While it may be difficult to think about investing for retirement when it is still a decade or more away, the results can be huge if you decide to plan ahead. For example, if you set aside just $1,000 per year in a retirement account that earns seven percent interest, then in ten years, that money will have grown to over $100,000. If that's what you make with minimum effort, imagine what you can do if you really put your nose to the grindstone. If you are planning on making real estate your primary focus, then having a few side investments already up and running is a great way to hedge your bets. Remember, an ounce of prevention is worth a pound of cure.

*B*onds

Bonds are a type of debt security, essentially a formal IOU. When purchasing a bond, what you are essentially doing is lending that money to the business or organization that issues the bond. This could be a state, corporation, federal agency, city, or other official entity. In return for this loan, the issues then agree to pay you interest on the loan for the life of the bond and then repay the principal on the date the bond is due.

*T*here are numerous different types of bonds, including US Treasury securities, corporate bonds, municipal bonds, asset bonds, mortgage bonds, sovereign bonds, and federal agency security bonds. You may also see bonds referred to as debt obligations, debt securities, notes, and bills though they all amount to the same thing.

. . .

*B*onds typically pay interest twice a year, which means they provide a secure and steady amount of income that you can set your watch and warrant on. They are not with risk, however, and determining the amount of risk is crucial to investing effectively in the long term. As a general rule, the riskier the bond, the larger the potential for profit and vice versa. The risk profile of a bond is multifaceted and includes tax status, credit ratings, default history, redemption features, maturity rate, yield, price, and interest rate. Altogether, these determine the value of the bond as a whole and whether it is the right investment for you.

*P*rice: The price of a bond is determined based on several distinct variables, including tax status, maturity, credit quality, liquidity, and supply and demand. Freshly created bonds typically sell at close to 100 percent of their face value. However, bonds are also traded freely in a secondary market where anyone can purchase a bond from anyone else for an equally agreed-upon price. When in the secondary market, the price of various bonds fluctuates based on changing factors, including supply and demand, overall economic conditions, credit quality, and interest rates. If the current price of a bond increases above its current face value, it is said to be a premium, and if it is listed below its face value, it is discounted. You will generally want to avoid purchasing bonds that are not near face value unless something about them warrants a diversion from this rule.

*I*nterest rate: Bonds generate interest that can be either payable at maturity, floating, or fixed. Fixed-rate bonds typically carry an interest rate that is determined when the bond is issued, and that is often expressed in terms of the overall percentage of the face amount. These payments are made twice a year. If the bond has a floating rate, however, the rate is periodically reset in line with the prevailing benchmark interest rates, which can be good or bad for the buyer depending on the current interest rates. Bonds whose interest is paid upon maturity are also known as zero-coupon bonds, and they typically sell for far less than the other two. Additionally, their price tends to fluctuate more in the secondary market.

*M*aturity: The maturity of a bond corresponds to the date on which you will receive full repayment of your initial purchase. Bond terms can be anywhere from one to thirty years. Short-term bonds mature within five years, medium-term bonds mature within twelve years, and long-term bonds mature within thirty years. Of the three, short-term bonds are typically considered the most stable because the repayment term is short enough to guarantee that most bond-issuers will still be around to honor their end of the deal. As such, they typically offer lower returns. The rate of return on bonds increases proportionately based on the length of the bond to compensate for market risks and pricing fluctuations.

*R*edemption features: While the rate of maturity determines how long a bond will generally remain outstanding, many bonds are also structured so that either the issuer or the investor can change the maturation date. This can typically be done through one of two means.

. . .

C all provisions require the issuer to redeem the bond at a set price and date prior to its full maturation date. A common example is when interest rates have dropped substantially from the issue date. When purchasing a bond, it is important to always inquire as to the possibility of a call provision. Bonds with this type of provision are preferable to purchasers as they further prevent undue risk, which means their premiums are almost always going to be higher than bonds without this level of protection.

A lternatively, a put provision bond provides the investor the option to sell the bond to the issuer for a set price prior to its maturation date. These types of provisions are typically exercised when the interest rate has increased dramatically, and the investor wants to reinvest in the bond at the new and improved interest rates. These types of bonds typically offer lower overall returns in exchange for this added benefit.

C *onversion:* Certain types of corporate bonds contain the option to receive payment of the bond in the form of stock instead of cash. These types of bonds will specify the details of this conversion, including when it will take place and how much stock they will be worth. These bonds typically have a lower rate of return as they offer the stability of a bond with the added benefit of stock.

A *verage life and principal payments:* Some bonds are traded and priced on the basis of their average life as opposed to their stated maturity. When it comes to purchasing bonds that are based on mortgage-backed securities, it is important to keep in mind that homeowners frequently prepay mortgages when interest rates decline, which can generate a principal return earlier than expected and thus reduce the overall timeframe of the bond and thus, the amount of interest it will generate. On the contrary, if mortgage rates rise, then the length of the bond can be extended beyond its original time frame.

Y *ield:* Yield is the amount of return a given bond is going to earn based on the interest payment and the price that was paid for it. Yield is typically written in the form of a percentage. Sub-units of this percentage are referred to as basis points. One basis point is equal to .01 percent. The bond yield comes in three types, yield to call, yield to maturity, and current yield. The current yield is the annual rate of return on the amount paid for the bond in the first place and can be found by taking the amount of the interest payment and dividing it by the price.

Y *ield* to maturity can be thought of as the overall return received if you hold the bond until it matures and is also known as the annual rate. This figure is associated with all bonds and allows you to compare bonds that are otherwise disparate. Yield to maturity is equal to the total amount of interest you are going to earn between the time the bond is purchased until it matures. This number would include all of the interest that is accrued, including any gains if it was purchased at a discount or losses if it was purchased at a premium.

. . .

*Y*ield to call is the total amount of return that will be received by holding the bond until it is utilized via a call provision. It is often also quoted in reference to the annual rate. Yield to call is determined in the same way that yield to maturity is an assumption that a bond will be called on the call date instead of the maturity date, as well as the fact that the investor will receive the total face value in addition to any other gains or losses.

*C*ash

While stocks and bonds should make up the majority of your investment portfolio, it is important to also keep some of your retirement plan in cash as well. This will allow you easy access to funds in case of an emergency without forcing you to alter your ongoing investments to get it. Determining the right amount of cash for your portfolio is tricky, however, as holding too much will come back to bite you if inflation takes a big jump while holding too little won't allow you to capitalize.

*I*t is important to keep in mind that if you are currently ten years or more away from retirement, it will often make sense to remain completely invested in equities such as stocks and bonds as the emergency fund will typically be enough to see yours through any immediate needs that you might have for cash in the short term. Above all else, it is important that your emergency fund is managed with capital preservation as the primary concern. Not taking risks with this money should be the most important thing, with earning a return as a secondary concern.

. . .

*U*ltimately, the right amount depends on you, your overall investment goals, and your tolerance for risk. In most situations, it is better to have slightly too little cash in your portfolio as opposed to slightly too much. The following steps can help determine the right amount for you.

- *Determine household cash and portfolio cash:* First up, it is important to keep the cash that you hold in your bank account separate from the cash that is a part of your retirement portfolio. This means that you are going to want to keep a sizable amount of cash as household cash, in addition to whatever your portfolio cash percentage is going to be. A good rule of thumb is to save enough on hand to allow you to pay for six months' worth of bills without having to tap into your portfolio. This could ultimately end up being a large part of the total net worth of investors who are still in the accumulation stage of their portfolio.

- *Portfolio cash:* Once you have separated your portfolio cash from your emergency fund cash, it is time to determine just how much of your holdings are currently liquid. Having too much cash in your portfolio creates what is known as cash drag in that the cash isn't actively doing anything besides accruing a low rate of interest. An average amount for many investors is somewhere between five and ten percent of their portfolio in cash. This, in turn, allows them to be ready for market events that will let them capitalize in a big way. This could include recessions or deep drops in the stock market, which can be capitalized on by those who have the funds standing by to do so.

- *Determine why you are saving the cash:* Instead of just looking at your portfolio, it is important to really analyze why you are currently keeping part of it in cash. Is the money a holdover from a sale that has not yet been reinvested? Is it there because you believe the markets are currently at a peak and a downtrend is on its way? Are you just waiting for the right opportunity to come along to capitalize on? If you have a valid answer to this question, then great, you are likely holding onto the cash for the right reasons. If the reason is more of an emotional one, then you will need to look long and hard at your finances in order to ensure you are not committing too heavily to cash.

If you find that your cash reserves are currently too large and causing a negative amount of cash drag on your portfolio, then you may want to divide that extra money into six equal parts and deploy part of it each month for six months. This way, you won't have to worry that it is all going too fast, and you can get a handle on your emotions between deployments.

MISTAKES TO AVOID

While there are some retirement-geared investing mistakes that you will only be able to learn to avoid via experience, a majority can be dealt with proactively, assuming you know about them beforehand. The following is a list of such mistakes. Remember, forewarned is forearmed.

Not Giving Enough Thought to Taxes

While thinking about taxes is never fun, the only other certainty in life is death, and you will need to think about taxes before then if you hope to live out the latter part of your life without simply counting the days until it occurs. After you retire, you are going to be solely responsible for ensuring you meet your tax requirements each year and ensuring that the money gets to the right agencies.

Taxes in retirement can have a drastic impact on the amount of income you get to hold onto as opposed to sending it off to a local or federal agency. As an example, your social security benefits will become partially taxable if the income you have available elsewhere is higher than a certain amount. If the bulk of your savings for retirement are in IRAs or a 401(k), then the money you withdraw from them on a monthly basis will count towards this limit. However, if some of your savings are in a Roth IRA instead, then those withdrawals won't count as income that can be taxed. While the specifics of how much you can count as income without issue will vary per person, the bottom line is that you will want to discuss these specifics with a financial advisor before you retire to prevent any nasty surprises once it is too late to do anything about it.

. . .

*R*elying Too Heavily on a Pension or Social Security

While the three-legged stool model will be enough to see some people through, relying too heavily on either social security or an existing pension plan can easily lead to less than ideal results later on. Regardless of how well provided for you feel you will be through these means, it is important to always have personal retirement plan investments to ensure that you will have what you need. There are always unforeseen issues that can arise with either of these two options, which means ensuring that you have yourself covered is always going to be the most reliable choice. After all, the worst-case scenario here is that everything works out fine and you have more money to enjoy in retirement, which is a situation anyone would be more than happy to find themselves in.

*P*utting Too Much Emphasis on Recent Events

Many people are prone to putting more emphasis on events that happened recently, even if they were essentially a fluke. For example, if your mutual fund provided an outstanding twenty percent return on investment last year and you expected it to do the same again this year despite the average being closer to seven percent over the past five years, then you are letting yourself fall into a bias based on recent events.

*R*ather than making this mistake, it is important to instead always focus on the average of all the events that have happened and avoid putting more emphasis on a particular portion of the data just because it is the most recent. The easiest way to ensure this is the case is to create your own investment policy statement and stick with it no matter what. This means you will want to have an answer to the following questions:

- How much risk are you willing to accept?
- How much are you investing, and where are you investing it?
- How long until retirement?
- What are your blind spots?

EARLY RETIREMENT GOALS

By and large, your plan for early retirement will look just like any other retirement plan. The biggest difference is, of course, that you have less time to put together all of the specifics. What's more, in addition to having less time to get everything right, you also have to ensure that the money you do put aside lasts for a longer period of time than you would otherwise need it to.

It is important to keep in mind that changing the timeframe will also change several other aspects of your retirement plan, though not all of them, and it is important to understand what those differences are going to be. The specifics are outlined below to ensure you don't enter into the increased time crunch blind, which means you will have a greater chance for success when it comes to making your dream of retiring early a reality.

WHY SHOULD YOU GO FOR EARLY RETIREMENT?

A vast majority of people retire in their sixties. You have to pay close attention to your investments and savings and also have discipline and a proper plan to retire early. However, the extra efforts and sacrifices that you need to put in are all worth the trouble. With early retirement planning, you can improve your financial footing and also rethink the things that bring you life satisfaction and happiness outside of your career. Here are a few reasons why you should go for early retirement:

*L*ower Spending and Consumption

Reducing your annual cost of living is one of the most constructive strategies for early retirement. To reduce your cost of living, you need to have a smaller retirement nest egg, which would allow you to stop working full-time earlier. In addition to that, decreasing your cost of living will also make you more conscious about your spending decisions and consumption. When you develop smarter habits of consumption, it would not only decrease your global footprint, but it would also be better for your pocket.

*P*rioritize Your Health

The consequences of a full-time career include firm time commitments, work travel, and commuting. Exercise often becomes secondary to your remaining daily responsibilities when you are working full-time. It is inherently unhealthy to sit in a chair for a major portion of the day. Also, office treats act as a constant temptation that can be harmful to your healthy eating decisions. Being healthy is probably one of the essential assets of our lives. When you retire early, you can put your health first, which would enable you to potentially extend your longevity and improve your overall well-being.

Travel

When you take vacations from work, they are seldom long enough. Travelling feels the best when there is no restriction on time. When you retire early, you can travel for extended periods, which is hard to do when you are working full-time. This will also prevent age from being a reason that could limit your decisions related to traveling. You can choose to travel by land, pass via several countries, volunteer in a disaster area, or spend a month or two in an interesting city—the opportunities to explore increases when your schedule is not restricted within a limited time frame. You can appreciate each destination in a better way through extended visits, which you might not be able to do with a quick tour stop.

Improve Your Relationships

You can have more chances to spend time with your loved ones if you retire early. Early retirees can make social activities their priorities rather than treating them as a slice of their schedules. You can enjoy the company of your family and spouse, and thus they can also benefit from the extra time. This does not mean that you will not be able to create strong relationships when you are a full-time employee. However, early retirement lets you dedicate more time to your loved ones. In addition to that, you can also be available to your family and friends who might require your help. Having freedom from your work schedule lets you help those in need, and that can be much more satisfying than creating status reports.

Certain Circumstances Might Require You to Seek Early Retirement

People don't always retire in the way they want. Some people might not be able to work at some point, which might make them retire. However, if you keep your finances and life prepared for early retirement, you can also be prepared in case you have to retire early. For instance, when the recession took place in 2008, a few older employees were forced to retire because they lost their job, and it was hard finding new jobs in a pool of younger workers. Another reason which could sideline a career is health ailments. It is particularly applicable for people working in professions that involve physical activities. Seeking early retirement can help decrease the difficulties that can arise when your working years are reduced for reasons that you cannot control.

Increase Income

When you plan to retire early, you will also realize that you need to have some extra income and make some sacrifices. Many people prefer to speed up their retirement savings because it is difficult to adjust to sacrifices. Planning for early retirement acts as a motivator for employees to work better at their present jobs to get more raises and promotions. Some employees also try to find other ways to earn money apart from their main source of income. Ideas for extra income can include real estate investments, a side business, or a second job.

GOALS THAT YOU SHOULD HAVE

Now that you know the different reasons why people choose to retire early, here are some goals you should set for your early retirement.

*B*uild Assets Faster

Traditional retirement investment planning emphasizes concepts like saving and passive investment strategies. These work great if you have somewhere between ten and forty years to get things right and need to plan for thirty or so years of retirement but work less well if you are going to speed up the time in which you need to successfully prepare. The traditional approach will only work with early retirement if you are planning to be extremely frugal in the long term in order to reduce the amount of income you will need and thus the amount of income you require.

*T*he big problem here is that a passive portfolio can only grow so fast, and it won't ever be fast enough for those looking to retire early and spend at traditional levels. The biggest killer to a traditional investment plan in this scenario is the loss of compound interest growth as a wealth-building tool. To compensate for this, you will need to add at least one of the following principles to balance things out.

*F*irst off, you can try being what is classified as an extraordinary saver. The level of frugality that is required in order to save enough to retire early through traditional means requires you to save approximately seventy percent of your earned income for anywhere from seven to ten years, depending on how much you make. While this is certainly possible, it is far from the ideal, which is why most people pursuing early retirement choose one of the other alternatives.

Second, you can try your hand at active investing. Active investing is defined as adding a component of skill to your investment strategies, which creates the opportunity for additional returns above and beyond what you can expect from passive returns. Ideally, you will want to double your rate of return, at the very least. This increased rate of return makes up for the loss of time when it comes to compound interest returns and balances things out to where they need to be. A good example of active investing is day trading as opposed to traditional trading.

Finally, you can use leverage to balance out the difference. This is done through either taking out a loan to jump-start your investments to levels not otherwise easily achieved or through investing in the foreign exchange market when investors can make trades with leverage included seeing huge returns for relatively small amounts of investment. However, it is important to keep in mind that both of these options require a good degree of risk, and if the investment decisions you make don't pay off, then you will be at an even greater disadvantage when it comes to retiring early.

A common way that many people go about utilizing leverage is through investing in real estate, as it offers business leverage, financial leverage, and tax advantages. Compared to other types of active investing, the learning curve is quite manageable. Regardless of the direction you chose to go, the formula is going to remain the same. Find a means of maximizing value through an unusual strategy or via enhanced skill and maximize the result to magnify the returns.

*A*ll told, there are three paths to wealth, real estate, business, and paper assets, and only two of the three offer the leverage you need to pursue early retirement without needing to worry about excessive frugality.

*B*e Aware of Inflation

Inflation is the term used to describe the continuous increase in the average cost of services and goods. As a consequence, the purchasing power of your dollar decreases. This means that for the same amount of money, you get lesser quantities of services and goods. It forms an indirect relationship. The value of money decreases as prices increase over time. The purchasing power decreases as inflation decreases. The causes of inflation can be explained by more than one theory. To prevent inventories from getting depleted, the prices of goods and services increases due to increasing demand. Cost-push is another such theory that explains the causes of inflation. In order to keep making a profit, companies have to increase their prices when the cost of production increases. Monetary inflation is another such theory. The price increases and the value of money decreases every time there is an oversupply of money. These theories offer a little perspective on the existence of inflation. However, they also show its permanence and highlight that it is a part of the economy.

. . .

*I*nflation can, thus, be thought of as cancer that destroys your savings from the inside. It can dismantle the wealth of those who plan to retire in a traditional fashion if they don't plan for it, and it will work much more aggressively on the wealth of those who plan to retire early if they don't take it into account from day one. A standard inflation rate of 4.5 percent will cut your purchasing power in half in about fifteen years, which means you will need to double your money in that time period just to maintain an even pace. What's worse, if you plan on retiring in your forties and hope to live until you are ninety, then you can expect to see this level of inflation three times in your retired life. When put another way, a dollar now will only be worth about ten cents after the third round of inflation is through with it.

*M*any fixed pensions and annuities don't account for inflation, which means they can't be counted on if you hope to retire early. As such, those striving for this goal are going to need to meticulously structure their portfolios and income sources with an eye towards offsetting the erosive effects of inflation. Great choices to stave off inflation include rental real estate, fixed income sources that adjust for cost of living increases, and equities.

*Y*our savings vehicle has to outdo inflation if it has to maintain itself and grow in value. If your retirement plans don't take inflation and the reduction in purchasing power into account, it will probably fail after some years. Here are some ways by which you can win the battle against inflation and protect your retirement income plan:

- Keep working even after you retire to collect the benefits that arise along with inflation. This can help protect you financially since your future benefits and retirement income might be calculated on the basis of the increased overall final salary.

- If you invest or keep investing in stocks after you retire, you can assist your retirement savings in keeping up with inflation. Even though no one can be sure that your stocks will outpace inflation, some evidence shows that "safe stocks" can perform well over long durations.

- Another method of keeping up with inflation is by purchasing real estate. To battle inflation in retirement, retirees should try to invest in real estate as it diversifies their sources of income.

- Delaying your social security payments can help protect you from inflation if you are in good health and have enough money to retire. Although these payments are protected from inflation, if you delay the payment, you can get a larger check later on, which will also be protected from inflation. However, this can change, so you also need to keep up with any legislation about Social Security benefits.

*T*ackle Spending Issues

Traditional retirement investment plans typically assume that you are going to see a marked decrease in spending as you get older. This is based on the idea that proportional activity level decreases as overall health and energy decrease. This decrease naturally offsets much of the impact of inflation and makes the overall spending picture fairly stable.

*T*he opposite is often true for those who retire early as these same studies show that spending typically increases and remains higher overall thanks to an overall healthier life coupled with a lifestyle that will remain active for twenty or thirty years before it starts to decrease. As those who retire early can't count on decreased spending to combat the dreaded inflation, they need to come up with other solutions when it comes to assuring financial security in the long term.

*F*irst, they can enter retirement with significantly more wealth than they need at the moment to provide them with a cushion to last as long as they need it to. Second, they can count on superior market returns to offset the difference. Third, they can supplement their retirement income via additional earned income from a part-time job. Finally, they can change their lifestyle in such a way that their expenses decrease. Ideally, you will want to mix and match at least two of these in your early retirement plan to ensure you can continue to make ends meet in the long term.

. . .

$\mathcal{A}$ study conducted by Ladder (a life insurance company) in 2019 revealed that an average American adult spends around $1500 every month on things that they can do without. That's almost $18,000 a year on non-essential items. This data seems baffling since almost seventy-eight percent of full-time American employees live paycheck to paycheck. One of the most effective ways to start saving for early retirement is by cutting back on spending. Here are some of the pointless things on which Americans should stop spending their money:

- **Impulse buying** – This includes anything that you are tempted to purchase, but you don't need it. Even though it might give you immediate satisfaction, the feeling will wear off even before you realize it.

- **Eating out** – A survey conducted in 2019 showed that out of almost 2000 Americans, sixty-nine percent reported that they spend money eating out. Even though it might feel good to go out and eat at a restaurant, the experience is not cheap. An average American spends around $750 on eating out every month and almost $9,000 every year.

- **Clothing and apparel** – According to the GOBankingRates report of 2019, an average American spends almost $1900 on clothes and apparel. Even though shopping for fast fashion appears very tempting, it doesn't take much time for whatever items are in style now to get replaced by something else. Therefore before you buy something, consider if you really need it.

- **Phone upgrades** – There's a hype every time a new smartphone from Samsung, Google, or Apple is released in the market, and it's hard to ignore that hype. However, today's smartphones are advanced enough to work properly for years, and even though the updated features are good, they are not life-altering. In the majority of cases, getting an upgrade only makes sense if your phone stops working or has major technical issues.

*M*ore Self-Reliance

Traditionally, retirement can be thought of as a three-legged stool with income coming in based on social security, savings, and pensions. For those who retire early, this will be reduced to two or even one leg, especially as pensions are fast going the way of the dinosaurs. Cutting social security out of the equation means that you are going to need to plan on being entirely self-reliant for at least a decade or more before Uncle Sam can swoop in and come to the rescue.

As such, it is important to budget for lower-income requirements until social security will kick in and make up the difference. At the very least, this means budgeting for increased insurance and health care costs until you finally do qualify for Medicare.

*P*erpetual Income Without Spending Principal

Ensuring your financial plan can support early retirement means ensuring that you have an income stream that you can't outlive; it is as simple as that. To understand the way in which extended time in retirement affects spending investment principal, it may help to use the example of a thirty-year mortgage. The initial mortgage payments pay off very little of the principal loan, and the later payments are practically all principal.

*T*he same is true when you are living off your assets in early retirement, the early payments will need to spend very little of the principal, and this amount can increase as time goes on. It is more difficult than with a loan, however, as you have no idea when the last payments will be.

*L*uckily, the process for planning for perpetual income is actually easier to determine than budgeting for a traditional retirement, though it is harder to put into practice. The assumptions and estimates that will be required when you create a traditional retirement budget all go out the window as early retirement is much more complicated and has a great many more unknowns. Instead, you can get a rough estimate of what you are going to need through four key rules.

. . .

*T*he first rule is that you will need to build an investment portfolio that is strong enough to allow for residual income in excess of your expected personal expenses. This doesn't mean actual return, just the extra that is generated by the assets that you own. You can only use this extra income; you can never touch the assets themselves if you want to be successful in this endeavor. This is a crucial distinction and one that cannot be overlooked or ignored. If the cash flow from your portfolio is greater than what you are regularly spending on living expenses, then you are essentially infinitely wealthy. Once this occurs, it doesn't matter how long you are going to live; this won't change.

*S*econd, you will need to ensure that you manage your assets in such a way that the growth you experience is greater than the rate of inflation. This means you are going to want to look into options such as properly valued stocks that pay dividends and real estate that generates a positive cash flow. Over time, these assets are more likely to grow with inflation rather than fight against it. As long as the results are greater than the inflation rate of 4.5 percent, then you can stop worrying about including inflation in your calculations; it will become a non-issue.

*F*inally, you are going to want to ensure that your residual income is coming from multiple sources that are non-correlated. Once again, a mixture of stocks that pay dividends and real estate that consistently creates income is enough to satisfy this rule. Additionally, you may want to mix in business income from a passive source for this rule. Things such as pension income, social security income, royalty income, and fixed annuity income all fit the bill.

. . .

*A*bove all else, it is important that you don't make the mistake of retiring early and basing your retirement around just one type of income. If this income source falls through for any reason, then you will have nothing to fall back on and will have to either cut back your lifestyle significantly or go back to work.

*F*inally, it is important to not make the jump to early retirement until your cash flow from passive income exceeds what you spend by a safe margin. This will make it easy to always have additional money lying around that you can reinvest in your future. This is a crucial level of insurance that is easy to over-look if you are too eager to begin your retirement. While it won't be necessary if the first three rules work out in your favor, it will be invaluable if the unforeseen happens and one of them falls through.

SAMPLE RETIREMENT PORTFOLIO

What follows are a number of sample retirement investment port-folios for your perusal. Hopefully, they will put you on the right track to ensuring your own successful retirement.

*I*ndividuals in Their Early Sixties, Financially Secure

This couple is a pair of public school teachers, the husband will retire in two years, and the wife will retire in four years. They both are lucky enough to retain traditional pensions, which, when combined with their social security returns, should be enough to cover their living expenses for the rest of their lives. They plan on supplementing their income via private tutoring and anticipate receiving a substantial inheritance when the wife's mother passes away. Combined, the couple has just over $700,000 in their 403(b) retirement plans.

$\mathcal{T}$his couple is in an enviable position all around. They don't need to deal with the risk of putting money into stocks because their portfolio is already strong enough to comfortably support them in their retirement at their current lifestyle. On the other hand, as they have their pensions, social security, and inheritance coming, they could also invest heavily in stocks without needing to worry about the additional risk.

$\mathcal{T}$hey could even go with a risky plan of 75 percent stocks and 25 percent bonds and still not have to worry about the outcome. While this is not the traditional model for older couples, it makes sense for them as they can see the market through any mild dips that it might take without worrying about their financial future. The additional returns that they receive as a result can be left to their children, grandchildren, or even to their favorite charities.

$\mathcal{S}$ingle Individual 59, Planning for a Simple Retirement

This individual has been divorced twice and is currently earning a modest salary as a medical technician. Thanks to a cash settlement from their second divorce and a substantial profit from a recent home sale, they have a portfolio that is worth nearly $900,000. They believe that they can live comfortably if they can manage to take $45,000 per year from savings and should ultimately be able to do so without any real problems as long as they invest smartly in the interim.

*W*hile this individual is nearly the same age as the individuals in the previous example, their situations are very different. This individual can only count on social security to supplement their income, which means they cannot afford to lose much money via risky investments. Assuming a modest return on their portfolio, they can expect to successfully retire within five years.

*A*s a fixed-income portfolio would be lost to inflation, in this instance, a fifty-fifty split between stocks and bonds would likely be a good choice when it comes to generating enough income for them to live for the next thirty or so years.

*Y*oung Individual, 29, Just Starting Out

This individual has just been out of business school for a few years and has earned an MBA. While they have a good job and a respectable salary, they are just beginning to build their savings. Their 401(k) currently has a balance of $3,700. Despite the obvious difference in their ages, this individual should most likely tailor their portfolio to look like that of the couple in the first example. This individual is still very far from retirement and doesn't anticipate any major financial roadblocks in the reasonable future.

*T*hey could even go with a more aggressive strategy of 80 or 90 percent stocks and ultimately come out just fine in the long term. Their 401(k) has plenty of time to grow and mature for close to four decades before it needs to support them. With that being said, they would still want a portion of their portfolio to be bonded to ensure a baseline level of stability. However, the first thing that this individual would need to do before investing heavily in anything would be to ensure they can pay for six months of expenses in case something unexpected happens. Once this is secured, they can then go about planning for the distant future.

*S*ingle Individual, 53, Hopes to Retire Early

This individual was never married and had no children. They dream of retiring early enough to travel the world and enjoy the experience. Currently, they have $75,000 worth of investments that are doing well. They are also saving a full 20 percent of their earnings each year.

*W*hile currently on the right track, this individual has a long way to go prior to realizing their dreams of early retirement and world travel. They find themselves in a tricky situation because the returns from bonds won't be enough to get her where she needs to be. While at the same time, her nest egg isn't large enough to warrant undue risk either. There needs to be a delicate balance here to ensure long term success. The best course of action is a portfolio that is about 30 percent bonds to ensure some stability with the rest in stocks to promote long term growth. As their situation changes, they will want to skew more towards bonds to ensure that the losses don't mount unduly.

RENTAL PROPERTY PRIMER

WHEN IT COMES to long-term retirement investments, there are few better choices than a rental property. As long as you have done your due diligence up to this point and have put together a nest egg to pull upfront costs from, rental properties can pay for themselves while also setting you up for retirement. What's more, they provide an emergency influx of cash if things don't go as planned and you have to liquidate at some point in the future. Other ways income-generating property investment payoffs include:

1. *Increase in asset value*

Inflation can quickly decrease the buying power of your income. The increase in value and revenue from property rentals, on the other hand, offers outstanding asset appreciation value. This is due to rental increases and improvements and better management of real estate rentals.

1. *Pride of property ownership*

*A*mong the many types of assets you can own, owning real estate generates the highest level of fulfillment. This is, however, dependent on finding the ideal location and ideal tenants.

1. *Meaningful investment value*

*R*eal estate is a highly profitable investment choice. Defined as a hard asset, the grounds hold value, the structure or buildings hold value, and the revenue received from rentals hold value. As the property is a physical asset, you can use this to leverage profit from more rental units or other investment types.

1. *Favorable returns as compared to stocks and shares*

*N*ot only do you receive better returns than the stock market, but real estate investment is not subject to constant change and upheaval influenced by external economic factors. For example, a natural disaster in Asia will not affect the value of the real estate you own on U.S. soil.

1. *Your investment is protected*

*O*wning stocks and shares offer little to no form of protection. If your investment in the stock market goes south, you could lose all of your shares portfolio value. With real estate investment, your land will always hold value, and then theirs is the protective cover of homeowners insurance.

1. *Leverage from a diversified investment portfolio*

*F*inancial investment experts expound on the many lucrative advantages of diversification. Through diversification, the risks are spread across many forms of investment

1. *Tax advantages*

*A*nother hugely popular benefit of investing in real estate is the advantageous tax benefits offered to real estate investors. Some of the tax benefits include deductions on:

- home loan interest
- monetary gains from real estate rental properties
- related costs and management and maintenance expenses
- property taxes
- property insurance and depreciation

7 WAYS TO TURN A PROFIT FROM RENTING OUT REAL ESTATE

The most common method by which real estate offers a profit is by increasing its value or appreciating. The method by which this is achieved is different for different kinds of real estate. However, selling is the only method by which it can be realized. On the other hand, there are several ways by which you can increase your return on investment. One method is to refinance the loan at a lower interest in case you borrowed money to purchase a property.

Through this, you can reduce your cost basis for the property and thereby increase the value you can clear from it.

*I*n the case of undeveloped land, the most common source of appreciation is developing it. When towns and cities start expanding, the value of the area outside its limits also increases as the potential for it to be bought by developers also increases. The value increases even further once the developers start building commercial buildings and houses. The discovery of commodities such as valuable minerals can also bring in appreciation of the land. This, however, holds true only if the buyer has the rights to them. Appreciation can come from natural resources such as trees, gravel deposits, etc. An extreme example would be striking oil.

*L*ocation often acts as the biggest factor when looking at residential properties. The value of a home increases as the neighborhood around it changes, adding playgrounds, shopping centers, schools, transit routes, etc. around it. This trend, however, also happens in reverse, with the values of homes decreasing as the neighborhood around them decays. Another way to spur appreciation is through home improvements. Remodeling a kitchen by installing state-of-the-art appliances, heating a garage, and adding an extra bedroom are some of the ways by which a homeowner might try to increase the home value. The method by which commercial properties gain value is the same as that of residential real estate and raw land: improvements, development, and location.

. . .

*I*nvesting in stocks offers only one avenue of receiving revenue, and this is dependent on the stock's appreciation value and the opportune timing of selling the stock. There are more ways than one to turn a profit from income-generating real estate.

Here are a few things to consider:

*I*ncome Generated From Rentals

This one needs no further explanation.

*B*uy a Property With a Low Market Value

Buying low is a widely practiced method. You can make a quick profit from selling real estate for more than you paid for it. Properties with a low market price tag include foreclosure. Of course, this method is made even more profitable if you have the required negotiation skill set.

*I*ncrease Market Value

Any improvements to the property increase its market value, allowing you to sell high. Unlike stock prices that are determined by the economic market, you have the choice of raising property value for higher returns.

*I*mproving Equity

Every mortgage repayment you make towards your property rental increases equity value.

Smaller Property Rental Units Can Yield More Returns Than a Larger Single Unit

By dividing one large-sized house into different units, you can rent these units out to a number of individual tenants and receive a larger sum in rent than just by renting out the house to one family.

Rent Out to Businesses

The market places a higher price tag on property rentals to businesses. The best commercial client is an established business.

Refinance Property to Improve Cash Flow

You can increase cash flow from property investment through refinancing. You can get more money into your pocket if refinancing allows for a decrease in mortgage repayments while the rental income you receive remains unchanged. The excess in cash flow received can be put towards the deposit for purchasing an additional property or saved for improvements or maintenance.

Your Success in Income-Generating Property Rentals Depends on You

This is perhaps one of the best reasons to invest in property rentals, as you are the critical factor in how well you do. You choose the area to purchase in, the type of property you want to rent out, the type of tenants you want to rent to (do you choose families or single professionals). Do you choose to buy a ready-to-move into property or a fixer-upper as you're so handy when it comes to property D-I-Y? Do you manage and maintain the property yourself, or do you outsource this to a property management company? How proactive are you in marketing your rental property and finding the best tenant?

*E*ven During Economic Turmoil, There Are Still Advantages to Owning Rental Property

Troubled economic times may not be all bad news for the property investor. There are potentially more people looking to rent, having lost their homes to foreclosure, and people being denied mortgage applications. And when the market stabilizes and improves, property prices will rise.

*A*s a Tangible Asset, Property Secures a Debt

If you've financed the purchase of property to generate income from it and for some reason you've defaulted on the repayments, you may lose the property and the income you receive from it but not your own house.

*T*he more knowledge and research you acquire before delving into real estate investment, the fewer fears you may have about what the future holds.

REAL ESTATE RENTAL BASICS

Investing in buy-to-let property is one of the sounder financial investments you can make, provided you do it properly. It can be a means of creating wealth that gives you financial freedom.

*T*he rewards can be exponential if you have an interest in educating yourself and learning new skills.

*H*ow Does Real Estate Investment Work?

Revenue-generating real estate investment works on a simple basic principle: positive cash flow – the income you receive must exceed outgoing expenditure.

*S*hould you sell or rent out? Renting out property for as long as you hold onto it will continue to provide you with revenue while its value increases. You can put any surplus income generated into acquiring your next property.

*B*uying real estate involves significant amounts of money, no matter what type you buy. And if you have to obtain a mortgage to buy your first property, this will be a long-term commitment to paying it off. The rental income you receive every month will have to cover monthly expenses such as mortgage repayments if you've had to finance the property and the related costs of managing and maintaining the property.

. . .

If You Can – Buy Cash

This is always the first preferred option as you do not have a financial burden hanging over your head.

How to Find the Capital for Rental Real Estate Without Your Own Money

Not everyone has the funds readily available to purchase real estate, but this should not stop you if you are determined. There are a few ways to secure a property rental if you look hard enough:

- Sell assets you do have, like your car, jewelry, or stocks and bonds.
- Find an investment partner.
- Get a loan privately.
- Take out a mortgage.
- Take over the mortgage payments of someone who is in financial distress and cannot afford it themselves.

Work Out the Financial Costs

If you do not have the full amount, the next best thing is to have a sizable deposit to put towards a mortgage. This can lower the monthly repayments you will be responsible for. Also, on taking a mortgage, you should be prepared to cover the costs for a few months while waiting for a tenant.

. . .

*T*he rent you ask for will depend on a number of factors, among which are the neighborhood and the type of property you have.

*H*ow to Determine the Best Rent Rate for Your Property Rental

The rent you ask for is the single-most-important determinant in your real estate investment endeavors. So how do you go about setting a rent rate that will provide you with the best returns and be attractive to potential tenants?

*T*he first thing to do is to find the reasonably-priced real estate you can afford. It is also advised to bear in mind that you should not look at investing in a rental property if the purchase price is twelve times more than what you expect to receive in rent for a year.

*A*t best, the rent you ask for will be an informed guess.

FACTORS TO CONSIDER WHEN CALCULATING RENT

Get an idea of what the going rental rate is for the area you are interested in. Deduct related essential expenses such as mortgage repayments, real estate taxes and insurance costs (remember to divide each of these cost factors by 12) and maintenance and repairs expenses (set aside a healthy allowance for these costs),

. . .

*A*void asking for too high a rent rate, or you may not find a good tenant easily, and your rental sits empty for a few months. At the same time, you need to make sure you don't underestimate what maintenance will cost you, and you end up paying more than you budgeted for.

*Y*our maintenance and repairs costs will depend on how old your property is, who your tenants are and how well they look after it (a house with young students may require more in terms of cosmetic repair than a house with more mature tenants). A third consideration is whether maintenance will be D-I-Y or outsourced to a contractor, or handled via a real estate management agency for a monthly management fee.

D-I-Y repairs mean lowered costs but the inconvenience of being available 24/7 should an emergency arise.

*F*inding the right balance between a fair market-related rate and a good value tenant, and you have found the perfect formula for consistent and favorable returns on your real estate rental investment for the long term.

*D*o Comprehensive Research

You need to conduct a thorough real estate search before you purchase your first buy-to-let property. In your search, you will need to base your choice on a number of factors. Chapter 3 is devoted to all those indicators that point to the desirability of a property rental. A good piece of advice is to look very carefully at the location. Even if the property looks a bit run down, but the area is great, it promises greater returns over the long term.

Start Off With One Property and Grow From There

Managing more than one piece of property can be overwhelming for even experienced landlords. Entering rental real estate is a learning curve and so starting off small makes sense financially and logically. If you have a basement, loft, or rooms to rent in your own home, you can start from here and then move on to buying real estate to rent out.

BEST PROPERTY TYPES TO INVEST IN

As a real estate investor, there is a varied choice of property types to choose from. As there are unique advantages and disadvantages to each, a useful suggestion is to choose the type that best fits in with your situation or needs.

There are some types of real estate that are more ideal for beginner property investors to cut their teeth on, so to speak. Here are a few suggestions on what type of property that offers favorable advantages.

Single-Family Homes

This is the most sought after type of property. Many new families or couples choose single-family homes as their preferred choice for long-term rentals. This type makes an ideal choice for a beginner investor as they offer better tenant quality value: financially stable, more likely to look after the property, and pay rent regularly. The single-family home is a detached property unit with a yard or driveway as a distinctive dividing line from neighboring properties.

dvantages:

- Improvements made can greatly increase the price you bought it for
- Provides greater returns on investment over the long-term
- Provided it is located in a thriving neighborhood with a good growth forecast, and it was well maintained, the property will hold a favorable resale value
- Property taxes are relatively lower as compared to multi-family units and commercial real estate
- Management costs are lower if you manage to secure a good quality tenant

isadvantages:

- Cash flow is dependent on one tenant only, unlike multi-family units. If a tenant moves out and you have to wait a while for another, the empty house will be a drain on your pocket

ulti-Family Housing

This type of real estate can be comprised of duplexes, triplexes, or quadplexes on a single plot, housing from two to four families. Each unit provides a rental opportunity. This type of real estate is easier to maintain and manage than having more than one single-family unit to look after.

dvantages:

- More financing options available for the investor
- If one tenant leaves, cash flow is still generated from the tenants of the other units
- If you, the owner, live in one of the units, you can benefit from the owner-occupied mortgage rate

isadvantages:

- The tenant pool for multi-family rentals is smaller, so there are few buyers when you do decide to resell
- Buying multi-family units are relatively more expensive than single-family homes
- Repairs may affect more than unit, especially if flooding is the cause

Condominium

A condo is a single unit in a larger building. The best advantage to opting to invest in condos is their low maintenance factor. In addition to this is the support of the condo association in sorting out any external repairs. Your worry is only to take care of interior repairs.

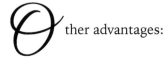

ther advantages:

- Large range of amenities available such as good security and recreational facilities such as fitness centers, swimming pool or clubhouse

isadvantages:

- Communal living
- Privacy is limited

FEATURES OF A PROFITABLE RENTAL PROPERTY

Here are some of the top features you should look into when searching for the right rental property:

roperty Taxes

Property taxes tend to vary across a particular region. It's not always bad if the property taxes are high as it can attract long-term tenants in a great neighborhood. However, some unappealing locations also have high property taxes sometimes. Thus, you might want to be aware of how much you will need to be paying and what you will be losing. You can talk to the homeowners you stay in the community. The assessment office of the municipality will also have all the information regarding the taxes on file. Also, make sure to find out whether property taxes could increase in the near future. If a town is in some kind of financial distress, the taxes might increase far beyond what a landlord can charge as rent.

Neighborhood

The vacancy rate of your property and the kind of tenants you attract will be determined by the neighborhood in which you purchase your property. If you purchase a property near a college or university, it is highly probable that your pool of potential clients will be dominated by students and that it could be hard to fill vacancies every summer. You also need to be aware that some towns don't encourage rental conversions by piling on red tapes and imposing extremely high permit fees.

Crime

If the area is a hotspot of criminal activity, no one will want to live there. There should be accurate crime statistics about the neighborhood with the public library or local police. Note whether criminal activity is declining or is on the rise, check the rates of petty and serious crimes and also vandalism. You can also ask about the frequency of the presence of police in the area.

Schools

If you are dealing with family-sized houses, consider the quality of the schools in the locality. Even though you will be mostly concerned about the cash flow per month, when you want to sell the property, the overall value of the property will be important. The value of your investment could be affected if there are no good schools near your rental property.

Job Market

Areas that have an increasing opportunity for employment will attract more tenants. You can visit a local library or check with the US Bureau of Labor Statistics to figure out how particular area rates as far as the availability of jobs is concerned. If you notice any news about a big company moving to a region, you can be sure that employees looking for a place to live will also move there. Depending on the kind of business, this might increase or decrease the prices of the houses.

Amenities

Take a tour of the neighborhood and check out the public transportation links, movie theatres, gyms, restaurants, parks, and all the different perks that might attract tenants. You might get an idea about where you can find the perfect blend of private property and public amenities from the promotional literature found in City Hall.

Future Development

Information regarding the plans that have been zoned into the region or regarding the development of the area will be available with the municipal planning department. It might be an area with a good chance of growth if there is a lot of construction going on. You also need to be aware of new developments that could decrease the price of the neighboring properties. In addition to that, new housing properties could also compete with your rental property.

TOP TIPS FOR BEGINNER INVESTORS IN RENTAL REAL ESTATE

What advice would seasoned investors or industry experts offer those just starting out as property investors?

- Look at real estate rentals as a long-term investment. This will provide you with greater returns on your investment.
- Start with a ready-to-move-in property. Fixer-uppers are ideal for those with some experience in property investment. Renovations usually take longer than expected and cost more than anticipated.
- When it comes to negotiating and purchasing, seek the experience of a professional real estate agent.
- Become an expert on the property market before your first purchase. Read up on trends, how to manage property rentals, etc.
- Consider being an owner-occupant as it can ease you into the responsibilities of being a landlord.
- Know your credit score before looking at acquiring finance.
- Investigate all your financing options thoroughly, including non-traditional approaches like hard money loans and real estate syndication.
- Start to build a network of contractors, suppliers, realtors, and other investors and landlords. You never know when you might need to call on one.
- It pays to be business-minded and to approach real estate investing like you would a traditional business. Take a business course if necessary to learn about the financial

terminology, accounting, and financial statements, and principles of building wealth.

- Have an exit strategy in mind. You don't want to focus on your real estate investment plan failing, but as the future is certain for no one, having a plan B will help minimize potential loss.

*I*n all your excitement, you may be tempted to head out and look for the first available buy-to-let property that looks profitable and sit back and wait for the rental income to pour in. The reality of real estate investment is far from being that simple.

*T*here is no escaping the time and effort in doing due diligence to choose the best property to rent out. Renting out real estate is defined by rules and regulations that you need to comply with, such as zoning regulations and permits. The best way to avoid making mistakes is to be aware of what they can be and not repeat them.

*L*earn from other landlords and real estate investors. Their knowledge and experience can be invaluable in saving you from the hassles and headaches many starter investors face.

KEY REASONS TO INVEST IN RENTAL REAL ESTATE

There are numerous benefits of investing in rental real estate. Investors can enjoy diversification, tax advantages, excellent returns, and predictable cash flow with the help of well-chosen assets. It is also possible to build wealth by leveraging real estate. Here are some of the benefits of investing in real estate and why it's considered to be a good investment:

Inflation Hedge

The positive relationship between the demand for real estate and the growth of GDP gives rise to the inflation hedging capability of real estate. The demand for real estate drives rents higher as economics keep expanding. This, in turn, gives higher values of capital. Thus, the real estate incorporates some of the inflationary pressure as capital appreciation. It also passes some of the inflationary pressure upon the tenants and thereby maintains the buying power of the capital.

Competitive Risk-Adjusted returns

The returns on real estate keep varying because of several factors, including management, asset class, and location. Several investors still try to beat the average returns of the S&P 500. Over the past fifty years, the average annual return has been calculated to be about eleven percent.

Real Estate Leverage

The term leverage is used to describe the use of different borrowed capital (i.e., debt) or financial instruments to increase the potential return on investment. For instance, a twenty percent down payment on a mortgage can give you a hundred percent of the property you wish to purchase – that's called leverage. Financing is readily available since real estate is a tangible asset and can serve as collateral.

*P*ortfolio Diversification

The diversification potential of real estate is another benefit of investing in them. They have a low or even a negative correlation with other kids of assets. This suggests that you can reduce the volatility of a portfolio by adding real estate to a portfolio of diversified assets. It can also increase the return per unit of risk.

*B*uild Wealth and Equity

You build equity as you pay down the mortgage of a property. It's an asset that forms a part of your total worth. When you continue to build equity, you acquire the leverage to increase your wealth and cash flow even more, as well as purchase even more properties.

*A*ppreciation

Real estate investors generate money with the help of rental income as well as appreciation and property-dependent business activities. The values of real estate generally continue to increase with time, and with the help of a good investment, you can gain profit when you decide to sell it. The cash flow also continues to increase over time as rents keep on increasing.

. . .

Tax Breaks and Deductions

Numerous tax breaks and deductions are advantageous to real estate investors since they can save money at the time of paying tax. Generally, you can remove the reasonable cost of managing, operating, and owning a property. In addition to that, you can benefit from several years of tax deductions that could reduce your taxed income since the cost of purchasing and improving a property cheapens over time. Another advantage is that you might be able to use a 1031 exchange and postpone capital gains.

Cash Flow

The net income received from a real estate investment after operating expenses and mortgage payments have been paid is known as cash flow. One of the main advantages of investing in real estate is its ability to create cash flow. In several instances, cash flow tends to increase over time as you build up your equity and pay down your mortgage.

BUILD YOUR REAL ESTATE TEAM

WHEN A HOUSE IS on the market, the door is always open. And not necessarily buyers are walking through.

*I*n most cases, contractors will emerge with a different mission regardless of whether it is spruce up the curb attraction, retile a bathroom, or take photos for the particular listing. So you need to ensure your checkbook is right.

A contractor is anyone that you employ for their services to get a particular job done right. Based on how much TLC your home demands, you could be looking for some of them.

*W*ith every contractor's special expertise, a house becomes easier to sell...but it won't be cheap. It is up to you to determine the kind of contractors worth the cost.

. . .

*W*ith the help of a real estate agent who has worked with every contractor, let us first look at this list for every contractor's job specs, pricing, and qualifications.

A COMPLETE LIST OF ALL CONTRACTORS REQUIRED TO SELL A HOME

Before diving into the little details, here is a brief summary of contractors required in a home sale and a short summary of what you need to expect from them.

- Real estate Agent-Markets and sells a home
- Real estate Attorney-Defends your legal rights when you sell a home
- Home inspector-verifies any problems with the structure of the home and its function
- Home Appraiser-Determines the value of your home
- Title agent- Reviews the title and offers title insurance to the lender
- Insurance Agent-Controls the homeowner's insurance for your move
- Mortgage Broker-Underwrites and services the mortgage
- Repair and maintenance contractors-as the name suggests, they fix and maintain the relevant repairs on your property
- Remodeling contractors – Take charge of cosmetic repair, installation, and updates for your home
- Real estate marketing Experts-Creates important tools and services to market and sell your home

That aside, what does a contractor do?

When you consider a contractor in a home sale, you perhaps think of a general contractor. This is the main contractor in a building project.

However, a contractor can be anyone who does work or delivers supplies. This means, if you sell a house, a contractor is anyone that you hire to complete the job. To simplify things, a contractor is a person who works based on a given contract.

The contract for each professional that you employ to work on your home sale needs to include the following information.

- Who, what, when, and where
- A job or service description
- The cost of the service
- The warranty information
- Terms of cancellation
- The process for settling disputes

*N*ow, let us dive deep into every contractor taking part in the home sale. We shall start with the most critical players.

*A*s a real estate wholesaler, you need a title company or title agent.

*W*hen a homeowner sells their home, the title company searches the title of the property to ensure that the title of the property is valid. The search shows whether there are any liens on the title to clear before the sale closes.

*I*n many cases, the title company will handle the escrow documents and support the closing of the sale with a settlement agent from the title company. The details of a title company, such as who selects the company and who can pay for the title insurance, change based on the state and county.

A typical title insurance policy features a one-time premium of around $1,000 that handles the upfront work and legal coverage. However, premium costs can extend from a few hundred to several thousand dollars.

*T*he contract between the seller and wholesaler will decide who covers the costs, and whatever costs you are accountable for will be reduced from your home sale proceeds during the time of closing.

*A*s a real estate wholesaler, you need a title company, appraise, and contractor to add a degree of profession-alism to your team and boost your full wholesale transaction. Each profession will save you time and money in the long run.

*T*he appraiser that will work with you can emerge on short notice and present to you an appraisal for the property you want to wholesale. This will make sure that you pay the right price for the property and have space in the price to resell the contract and generate profit. An experienced buyer may also want to see the appraisal before you buy the property.

*G*etting a reliable and sensible contractor improves your business. The contractor can come with you to search for the possible property and can draw up an estimate of repairs. You may not know that this is important because you are not fixing up the property, and you are selling it 'as is' condition. However, it is important when you get a buyer.

*Y*ou can find all these three professionals through referrals, recommendations, and online searches in real estate wholesaling groups. Another real estate wholesaler can tell you who he recommends in your area.

PICKING THE CORRECT TITLE COMPANY

Purchasing a property is one of the biggest and most critical parts of a consumer. As a result, it is important that a genuine title company is selected to carry out the transaction. This is vital when an individual is selling or acquiring a mortgage on their home. It is important that a consumer picks up the right title company to deal with the closing.

HOW TO GET A TITLE COMPANY?

Just because a company has signed on the door showing that they are a title company doesn't imply that they are the right choice. There are a lot of things that you need to consider in a title company:

- *Reputation and longevity* - Find out from your realtor or even lender about the company. Does it have a track record for proficiency and competency? For how many years have they been in business? Check the website of the company and search it online.

- *Location convenience and ability to accommodate the customer* - Is the seller and buyer in separate places? You want to make sure that the Title company will cooperate with you to schedule your closing at a mutually convenient time and location.

- *Price is a major factor* - Simply because a company might provide lower title insurance rates and closing charges doesn't imply it is the best choice.

- *Competency and level of professionalism* - When walking into the office, does it look harried? How are the employees dressed, and do they act professionally? Is the workplace organized? What is the level of experience the company's title examiners and closing agents have?

- *Customer-oriented.* How did they make you feel when you first entered the place?
- *Legal support* - Most established title companies contain in-house attorneys, which is a great thing for you. They quickly address closing problems and title challenges to eradicate a title or closing issue.

- *Multi-faceted and professional membership* - How capable is the company in dealing with 1031 exchange, email closing documents, and many more? Is the company technologically capable?

TITLE INSURANCE

Once the title is established to be genuine, the title company will produce a title insurance policy. This will cover the lenders or owners against claims of legal fees that may emerge from disputes over property ownership.

Whether you are a seasoned investor or a wholesaler, working with an investor-friendly title company will boost your chances of success.

So far, you know what a title company is, but there is a huge difference between an investor-friendly title company and one that doesn't offer services to investors.

Many title companies carry out normal closings day in and day out, which often requires a person purchasing a home via a realtor and getting a mortgage. However, most of them aren't used to Assignment Agreements, Back to Back Closings and Double Closings. This is the reason why it is important for you to identify an Investor-Friendly before you go out and put your first house under contract.

Therefore, your first role as a real estate wholesaler is to look for a Superhero Title Agent that works together with investors regularly.

Normally, in real estate transactions, "issues" arise with the title, errors in records, missing heirs, illegal deeds, and the list go on. A huge title agent will uncover and eliminate these problems and save your deal from moving south.

. . .

*O*nce you find your superhero title agent ensure that you appreciate them by dropping a thank you card in the mail. Small gestures go a long way with persons who feel over-worked and underappreciated.

THE STEPS OF A TITLE PROCESS

1. *Beginning the Process* - A sales contract is sold between you and the seller, and then you will send it to the title company. The escrow is accepted with the title agent and always confirmed using an earnest money receipt upon request. The escrow agent begins the closing process by opening a title order. The file starts to be processed using a collection of data but is not limited to finding loan payoff information, legal documentation for formal entities, and ordering inspections.
2. *Title Search and Examination* - This search is carried out in public records. The records comprise mortgages, assessments, wills, judgments, divorce settlements, and other documents that change the title to the property. Title examination involves an analysis of documents presented during the title search that impact the title property. This step confirms who the legal owner is and the kinds of debts owed against the property determined.
3. *Document Preparation* - The closing agent will examine the lender's documents and instructions, respect the real estate contract terms and agreements, type the correct documents, evaluate instructions from other parties taking part in the transaction, and place closing fees into the settlement statement. The escrow agent works as a major

communicator with all parties involved in the entire process until it is ready to schedule and close.

4. *The end buyer wires funds* - A day or two before closing, your end buyer will wire the fund for closing to the title companies account.

5. *Closing of the transaction* - The settlement agent oversees the closing transaction: the seller signs the settlement statement, and the owner's affidavit plus the miscellaneous closing documents. The buyer will sign the final CD and their settlement statement.

TIPS TO GET AN INVESTOR-FRIENDLY TITLE COMPANY

First, you must know what you look for: First off, carry out some research to learn what the title company does and how it operates within the web of wholesalers, buyers, sellers, and investors.

he basic responsibilities of a title company

- Make sure that the titles to properties are genuine.
- Follow closings
- Release title insurance for properties

nvestor friendly title company

- Know about wholesaling
- Carries out double closings
- Specializes in working with real estate investors
- Has a great reputation.
- Creates a relationship with you

Don't just look up companies: When you want to get the best title company from a long list is like looking for a needle in a haystack. There is a lot to select from, and many of them don't tick the checkboxes for being investor-friendly.

You need to involve other resources at your hand to complete the search process. Some of these resources include wholesalers, investors, and REIA groups around your market.

Speak to other investors and wholesalers with good experience: Interacting with people who have worked in real estate investing for a long time is the best means to access important information.

Ask for recommendations on social media pages followed by wholesalers. Look for these pages using a quick Facebook search.

· · ·

ecome a member of an REIA group and get in touch with other members: There are a lot of real estate investor networks and clubs in your location. Be a member of one to get a periodic newsletter with lots of helpful information.

inally, most investor meetings include title companies that pay to get sponsorship. They will be versed with investors' needs. Not only will you have access to a wealth of information as a member, but you will also get in touch with mentors who can direct you through your journey in real estate investing.

onnections and connections: Besides being a member of an REIA group, you need to attend meetings and take advantage of opportunities to network. Speaking face to face with another person demonstrates your dedication and delivers the perfect opportunity for investors to link you up with the title companies they trust. Meetup.com always has up to date information about general meetups.

e inquisitive: You might need to represent yourself when you get a title company, and this can work against you if you are a newbie and not so sure about what you are doing. When you get in touch with prospective agents, lookout for more information.

ome of the questions that you should consider asking include:

- How much do you know about wholesaling?
- Do you work with investors?
- How often do you carry out double closings?
- What other forms of transactions are you experienced in?
- Who else can recommend you to me?
- Can you manage to work with tight deadlines?

*W*orking with a company that is both credible and understanding as an investor will make closing deals easier.

*N*ow that you have all the tips that you need to start searching for a title company. What are you waiting for?

FIND YOUR ROLE IN YOUR REAL ESTATE TEAM

Having secured an able title company, the next most important task is to consider your role in the company. Having a team can share the responsibilities, only when the duties are ruled out, that includes you - the boss, as well.

*T*o assign yourself a duty, consider all your strengths and weaknesses. Consider all the areas of your expertise and take responsibility for that role. Since you are building a team, you need to use your strengths to their absolute potential.

· · ·

*D*o not overlook your weaknesses; consider them as well. You might be good at many things and bad at a few, but a good team leader will consider both points. Being well aware of one's weaknesses can prove to be beneficial while working on building a team of their own. How? Well, if you know the sectors that still need polishing, you can simply hire people who are experts in those areas.

*W*orking on the areas that still need refining can cost you both time and money. Since you are already looking forward to building your real estate team, the best way out is to fill in those gaps with people who are already experts in those respective areas. That way, not only will your team get stronger, but you too will get to learn and improve yourself without hampering the work process. After all, what is a team for? A team not only elevates the workload off of your hands but also improves the overall working in the respective field.

WHO ARE THE PEOPLE YOU SHOULD HIRE ON YOUR TEAM?

Having figured out your role in the company, now is the time to focus on the people whom you should hire. You might follow these steps to help you have a clear picture of the list of employees you might need on your side:

- *The Supreme Goal of Your Company* – This is the most important point to consider before moving on to the recruitment process. You need to fix a goal for your team. If your goal is commercial real estate oriented, then you might need a different set of people in your team than if you are planning to work on real estate investments. Having a clear vision of the ultimate goal will not only help you enlist the set of people you might need on your array but will also ease out the entire process. Even if you have more than one ultimate goal, list them down. You might want to invest in apartment buildings and also locate and fund in buildings, consider both the goals carefully and study the set of people required for both the projects for the smooth working of the team. At the end of the day, your goal will directly impact the crew that you might need.

- *Special Expertise Requirement* – Having decided upon the ultimate goal, now is the time to consider special requirements. You might have to recruit contractors, lawyers, brokers, and many other people, but you feel vulnerable. In that case, you might want to recruit someone who is an expert in the area of picking the best people from the queue.

- *Watch and Learn from Other Efficient Teams* – It might prove to be one of the most important steps towards building a scalable real estate team. Take time to observe and learn from other teams around you. Observe their work ethics and pick the best from them. Watch the team structure, the strengths, and expertise of their team, that will help you understand how a dedicated team functions. Make sure to learn from their strengths and weaknesses and take note of things that might be changed to make your team better than the rest.

- *Test Period* – A person might seem extremely enthusiastic and dedicated to their job during the initial process, but once they are hired, they may turn out to be trouble. Having them removed and running the entire process of interviewing again to fill the spot is an absolute waste of time. Instead, you might allot a probation period. During this period, you monitor the employees and judge whether or not they fit the bill. You can then hire those who are interested in working for your team. The employees benefit from this as well since they get to learn your company's work ethics and decide whether or not to stay in the place.

These points will help you get a list of all the people you will possibly need on your team but give you a head start; here is a list of members that are required in every team regardless of their goal –

1. *Attorneys* – They are the lawyers that you must have on your team to take care of all the legal bills and documentations.
2. *Administration* – Also referred to as assistants, are the first people who get contacted by potential clients for business-related queries.
3. *Listing and Marketing Specialist* – the ones who generate

leads, manage your advertising and PRs, and other related jobs.

4. *Human Resources* – The HRs are responsible for diversifying your team and hiring members who add more value to your team.

FINDING THE RIGHT PROPERTY

FINDING THE PERFECT AREA

THE FIRST THING you will need to do when it comes to finding a property that is worth your time is narrow down your search to a specific area. The easiest way to start is by looking at the price of properties in a specific area as well as what properties in that area are currently renting for. Once you find a few areas that seem promising, the next thing you are going to want to do is to get out there and take a look at the areas in question for yourself. You will want to visit the area both during the day and again at night to really get a feel for it and ensure that the feel of the place doesn't dramatically change between the two.

When you are there, you are going to want to try and talk to a few locals to make sure you get the real scoop on the area. The best type of people to talk to is current renters, as homeowners have a vested interest in the area, which might skew your results. You will also want to visit a local police station and ask to see local crime records so you can determine the level of crime in the area, which is often a good indicator of its overall quality.

Based on these results, you will then want to consider the type of individuals who may be attracted to the area so that you can determine what local amenities exist that might make it more attractive for them. Schools and parks are an asset to family neighborhoods, while access to nightlife or quality jobs are of interest to young professionals. Additionally, once you have found out the classification for the area in question, you can keep an eye on the local news and town hall meetings for incoming changes to the area that might make it more or less attractive.

Secondary cities: When it comes to finding the best value to price ratio, the best place to start isn't with the real estate markets that are currently seeing lots of real estate action. It is instead to look to places that are a step removed from the hot spots if you hope to find the best bargains. Known as secondary cities, these areas are primed for a major real estate boom in the relatively near future, which means you need to act quickly if you want to get in while the getting is good.

To start, you may find it helpful to understand what parts of the market are on the table when it comes to considering secondary market cities. The most active real estate cities in the US are known as global cities, those such as New York, Washington DC, Baltimore, San Francisco, Los Angeles, Chicago, and Boston, and transactions there make up approximately 50 percent of all the real estate transactions that happen in the United States each year. From there, you have other major cities that have large populations, 5 million or more, places like Miami, Florida, Dallas, Texas, and Phoenix, Arizona.

With those out of the way, you get to the secondary cities, places that have more than three million residents but less than five million and that are currently in the midst of or on the cusp of a substantial real estate boom. This all combines to ensure that these areas offer up a wealth of possibilities for the potential real estate investor as the lack of investor demand means that prices will naturally be lower.

If you are hoping to take advantage of a secondary city, it is important to keep in mind that going to regions that have already been identified as such misses the point of the secondary city entirely. Most cities will not maintain their status in a particular tier indefinitely, which means it is important that any research you do into the topic is as up to date as possible.

FIND THE BEST DEALS

MLS

The first place that you are going to want to look when it comes to finding houses that are underpriced is the same place that everyone else is going to start, and with good reason. The Multiple Listing Service is a compilation of every single property that is currently being represented by a licensed real estate agent in the United States. The competition on this site is going to be extremely fierce, but that doesn't mean that you won't be able to score a great deal every now and then as long as you are willing to work for it.

First things first, this means that you are going to want to check the new listings very early in the morning (4 a.m. eastern standard time early) and again before you go to bed every night. You will always want to pay special attention to properties that are listed on Fridays as they are typically going to have less competition simply due to the fact that people don't like to work on Fridays. Additionally, you are going to want to be persistent on listings that seem difficult to get a hold of; remember, if you are having trouble, so is everyone else, which means most people are going to give up before getting anywhere. Persevere, and you never know what you might find.

You never know when a great deal is going to pop up, but be sure that it won't last long once it does. This means that as soon as you do come across a deal that you won't be able to pass up, you are going to need to be able to act on it as quickly as possible. Contacting the listing agent promptly is key, as is being able to drop everything and view the property as soon as the real estate agent or the owner is available. When you do go to see the property, it is important that you take a real estate inspector with you if you don't know what type of serious issues to look for. You don't want to have to schedule a second showing before making an offer; strive to get as much done all at once as possible.

When you are scouring the MLS listings, it is important to keep an eye out for properties that have been on the service before that have been taken down, only to reappear suddenly. This means that the original deal for the property has fallen through which, in turn, means that the owners are going to be more willing to negotiate as they will typically be losing faith in the system that saw a deal fall through once it was on the verge of completion. These types of sellers are likely going to be on the lookout for a way to finish the process as quickly as possible, which means you can stumble into an exquisite deal if you are preapproved and ready to go. In these situations, speed is going to be even more of a factor than normal as the first person who is prepared in such a way is often going to win the day.

Additionally, there is always the chance that you will simply get lucky. There are hundreds of new listings added to the MLS every day, often in your area alone, which means you are just as likely to stumble across a good deal as not. Sometimes you will be able to come across a short sale early enough that you can snatch it up before another investor, or the sellers might simply have priced their property below its current value because they need it to sell as quickly as possible. Think of the MLS as gambling; if you don't play, you can never win.

Foreclosures

While inexperienced investors are often urged away from trying to make money on foreclosed properties because there are numerous different variables involved, those who approach them with the proper strategy can actually make a decent amount of extra profit while working in the foreclosed space. For starters, it can be helpful to have foreclosure defined as it has a few different meanings and can also mean different things in different states. Officially, foreclosure is the name given to the entire process where the holder of a lien takes legal ownership of the property in question when a loan tied to that property is defaulted upon.

The specifics of the entire foreclosure process are going to vary by state, but they all typically include a period where the lienholder is still trying to get the property owner to pay what they owe without taking expensive legal action. When it comes to buying a property in foreclosure, you can actually do so at three separate times and still make an extra profit; they are during the period of pre-foreclosure when the lienholder is still just threatening action, the last minute before the lienholder acquires the property and after the lienholder has purchased the property, though this last one isn't recommended if you hope to find the best deals possible.

The methods that work for finding homes that are in the pre-foreclosure state will vary depending on the area that you are looking to purchase property in and will all require a good bit of research, though the results will certainly be worth it if they work out in your favor. First, you are going to want to visit the county court-house nearest the area that you hope to purchase property in. While there, you are going to want to look into any Notices of Default that have been filed against loan holders in the recent past. While not all of these loans will be related to property specifically, it is still a great place to check.

If the results from your search are found wanting, the next place you will want to go is the county recorder's office as much of their information is only available via a closed system, which means it is the place to go if you need to go deep. Here you will want to search for real estate data or court records that are related to notices of default. You will also want to look for judgments against property owners or issues related to liens on the property.

Finally, you might be able to find some of the information that you are looking for by simply keeping an eye on any local newspapers that are still slouching along. The legal notice section of the news-paper will occasionally include information pertaining to notices of default if the lienholder hasn't been able to otherwise serve the borrower with details of the legal action that is being taken. Addresses are usually included in these notices, which makes them a great way to find leads on individuals who might be open to selling before the foreclosure process proceeds any further.

Individuals that you track down using this information are often very eager to negotiate as allowing things to go farther with the foreclosure process means they get less than they otherwise might, even from a lowball deal. If you approach a potential seller under these conditions, it is important that you always have cash on hand or access to a preapproved or hard money loan, as once you have the homeowner onboard, you are going to need to close the deal as quickly as possible before they have time to overthink things and hold off in hopes of getting a better deal. The goal is to provide the easiest answer possible as quickly as possible; otherwise, the quality of the deal is likely to decrease significantly.

Courthouse Steps Auction

While they don't take place everywhere, in many areas, once a lien-holder forecloses on a property and the foreclosure has been completed, the final step in the process is for the property to be auctioned off. While they do not always take place on the court-house steps, these auctions are a great way to pick up the property on the cheap, though you will not always be able to get a good read on the property beforehand. Details regarding these auctions can be found in the local paper or online on the county or city website. Bidding typically starts at the amount that was owed on the property when it was foreclosed on so that the lienholder can earn their money back if not necessarily turn a profit.

The amount of information that you are able to track down about the property in question is going to vary from sale to sale. If you can track down the details regarding the individual properties beforehand, then you can mitigate a good deal of the potential risk, though this will not always be readily available. Greater risk leads to a greater potential for reward, however, and this type of sale can frequently lead to the ownership of properties that you could otherwise never be able to afford, given your current budget. If you come across a price that is absolutely too good to pass up, be aware that you are going to need to have a preapproved loan ready and waiting or cash on hand as the sale won't wait for you to take care of these sorts of things after the fact.

TAKE A DRIVE THROUGH THAT FRIENDLY NEIGHBOURHOOD

We are all guilty of rejecting the best deals simply because they were not in an area of our choice. If you have any particular neighborhood (s) in mind where you wish to buy your property, then simply drive through the area.

Taking a short drive through the neighborhood can turn out to be fruitful as more than often latent sellers put their properties on sale by simply putting up the sign 'for sale". They are doing this to test the waters (meaning market here) before they finally move on to take greater measures, like going to real estate agents or putting up an advertisement.

When you find a property for sale in this manner, you need to be quick in making a decision for or against the property. These properties with "for sale" signs stay in the market for a max period of a month. After that, you cannot buy these properties directly from the owner as they have already gone to a real estate seller or are sold.

This measure is taken by sellers to sell off their property quickly and in a hassle-free way due to any personal reason. The prices will be lower; also, there will be no third party involvement. Thus, giving you the best possible deal.

INTERNET SCOURING

Internet technology has become an integral part of our everyday routines. There is absolutely nothing that you cannot find on the Internet – starting from vegetable and fruit shopping to job vacancies to buying gadgets - everything can be found on this giant platform. No wonder even the real estate business has not escaped from the impact of the internet. Thus scouring the Internet can help you find the right property in the US.

You will find a number of websites that list thousands of properties and their details, and you will have to go through them all. There is a drawback in flipping through websites. In the United States, websites do not sell or enlist real estate properties on a national level. They are more state-based. This can prove really difficult if you are not computer savvy and are not aware of which website is related to which state. Even if you do know the websites and their related states, it can be difficult to remember them.

The best way to cope with this situation is to visit certain sites that collect information from all other websites, regardless of their state, of realtors (even the ones that are the best) and present a list of all the eligible properties depending on your description. All that you have to do is mention all your requirements, including area or location of preference, price range, and property area, and all the eligible candidates will be presented to you under the same virtual shade.

As you can already conclude, this is the most convenient way of finding your dream property as it saves time, energy, and traveling expenses. Also, sites that collect information from all other websites always remain updated about the most recent property listings, thus giving you a plethora of options to choose from.

It is possible that most of such websites have a mobile version as well to give you the best experience if you do not have a MacBook or laptop. Applications can also be installed. Most people in the United States (about 77%) find their dream properties through this method only.

But there are certain things that need to be considered in this mode of purchase to save oneself from the wrath of catfish. You must physically visit and take a look at the property before finalizing it (many times); images may vary from the real property with respect to size. Few cases have also been registered where the property was completely different from what was displayed on the website. Thus, as convenient as it might seem, you might still want to visit the location and take a careful tour of the property before finalizing it.

CONTACT REAL ESTATE AGENTS

Unlike other countries, in the United States, in order to become a real estate agent, they need to pass exams, thus making them knowledgeable in every aspect of real estate dealings, which includes all related rules and regulations.

When you are hiring a real estate agent, make sure they are licensed and not an impostor. A licensed agent is an expert who has knowledge of all the potential properties up for sale in their respective states and also has a list of all the properties that will be for sale in the next few months. They are going to benefit you greatly in your hunt for the right property and in the right area.

Even if all the above-mentioned techniques fail you, hiring a real estate agent will ensure that you find the right property. However, make this your last resort, as hiring an expert can be heavy from a monetary perspective.

GETTING A GOOD DEAL

NEGOTIATION STARTS with the universally applicable rules. These rules demand people be understood and accepted. One way this can be achieved is through listening. By listening, you demonstrate empathy and an open desire to find out what the other party is experiencing.

WHAT MAKES A GOOD NEGOTIATOR

The best negotiators are always ready for surprises. Great negotiators employ their skills to express the surprises they are sure to exist.

*G*reat negotiators challenge the assumptions that others trust on faith or in arrogance. As a result, they remain open to all opportunities and more intellectually agile to any situation.

. . .

People who consider negotiation as a means of arguments are always overwhelmed by the many voices in their head. Negotiation should not be a fight; it is a means of discovery. Your purpose should be to discover as much information as possible.

To silence the voices in your head, focus on the other party and what they say.

Your main focus should be to find out what your other party wants and allow them to feel safe to talk about whatever they want.

Negotiation should start with listening, let it be about the other person, validate their feelings, and build trust and safety for an actual conversation to start.

Taking it too fast is one of the greatest mistakes that many negotiators make. If you are in a hurry, people may start to think like they are not being heard and you risk affecting the rapport and trust you have established.

BE AWARE OF YOUR TONE

1. *The late-night FM DJ voice:* Use this voice selectively to emphasize a point. Lower your voice, ensuring that it remains calm and slow. When done correctly, you build an

aura of authority and trust without generating defensiveness.

2. *The positive voice:* This should be your default voice. It is the voice of a good-natured individual. Your attitude should be light and encouraging. The main thing here is to relax and smile while you are talking.

3. *The assertive voice:* Used scarcely. Will trigger problems and build a pushback.

*W*ear a smile on your face. When people have a positive state of mind, they think faster and are likely to work together and solve problems. Positivity builds mental agility in both you and the counterpart.

*Y*ou can decide to be very direct and to the point as long as you ensure safety by a tone of voice that shows you are okay.

*L*ook at assumptions as hypotheses and apply the negotiation to measure them thoroughly.

*R*epeat the last three words of what a person says. You always fear what looks different but are attracted to what is similar. Mirroring is the act of insinuating similarity, which activates bonding. Use mirrors to let the other party emphasize and bond with you, keep people talking, create time for your side to regroup, and assist your counterparts in disclosing their strategy.

*B*y repeating what people say, your other party will explain what was just spoken and support the act of connection.

*I*n a certain study, the average tip of the waiters who repeated back was 70 percent more than those who applied positive reinforcement.

*H*aving the correct mindset is the main factor in a successful negotiation.

DON'T JUST FEEL THEIR PAIN, BUT LABEL IT

Tactical empathy involves understanding the feelings and mindsets of the other person. Try to learn what is behind those feelings so that you can spread your influence in all the moments that come. It's generating attention to both the emotional barriers and the possible pathways to ensure an agreement is made.

*W*hen you closely look at another person's face, tone of voice, and gestures, your brain starts to align with theirs in a process described as neural resonance, and that makes you understand what they feel and think.

· · ·

*I*f you want to speed your neural resonance skills, take some time now and practice it. Focus your attention on an individual that is talking to you, or watch someone being interviewed on TV. As they speak, assume that you are that person. See yourself in the status they describe.

*L*abeling is a means of validating someone's emotion by accepting it. Assign a name to your buyer's/seller's emotion and ensure you identify their feelings. It gets you closer to them without requesting external aspects you know nothing about.

*T*he first step to labeling is identifying the other person's emotional state.

*T*he way of highlighting feelings is to pay close attention to changes in their experience when they respond to external events. In most cases, those events reflect your words.

*O*nce you identify an emotion that you want to specify, the next thing is to label it aloud. Labels can be described as statements or questions. The only difference is whether you finish the sentence with a downward or upward inflection.

*R*egardless of how you end, labels always start with basically the same words:

- "It sounds like...."
- "It looks like...."
- "It seems like..."

When you respond, your colleague will often give a longer response than just "yes" or "no." And in case they disagree with the label, that is fine. You can always step back and say, "I didn't mean that was what it was. I only said it looks like that."

The last rule governs labeling is to focus on the underlying emotions. Labeling negatives corrupts them in extreme instances. Labeling positives enhances them.

Labeling is important because it de-escalates angry interactions because it makes the individual acknowledge their feelings instead of continuing to process them.

The fastest and most effective method of attaining a quick interactive relationship is to accept the negative and diffuse it.

Research has demonstrated that the best approach to handle negativity is to observe it without judgment and reaction. Then consciously label every negative feeling and substitute it with positive, compassionate, and answer-based instincts.

. . .

*A*ssume yourself in your colleague's situation. When you accept the situation of the other person, you quickly demonstrate that you are listening; they can mention to you something that you can use.

*T*he reasons why the other party may fail to agree with you are always more strong than why they will make a deal. As a result, you need to concentrate on eliminating the obstacles to an agreement. Denying negative influences offers them credence. It places them into the open.

*O*nce you label an obstacle or mirror a statement, allow it to sink in. Don't be scared; the other party will speak while you are silent.

*L*abel the fears of your counterpart to diffuse their power.

*O*utline the worst things that the other party can say and say them before the other person can. Since these accusations usually appear exaggerated when spoken loudly, speaking them will motivate the other party to say that the opposite is true.

*K*eep in mind that you are interacting with a person who wants to be acknowledged and understood. So you need to apply labels to enhance and encourage positive perceptions and dynamics.

UNDERSTAND THAT YES AND NO ARE JUST WORDS

Forcing a "yes" doesn't convince a negotiator to accept, but it only annoys the opposite side.

*T*he best negotiators are aware that "no" offers a chance for you and the other party to make it clear what you want.

*I*n other words, "no" is the beginning of a negotiation, but not the end of it.

*T*he best negotiators aim for "no" because they are aware that it is always when the initial negotiation starts.

*S*ometimes, "no" may mean:

- I don't understand
- I want a different thing
- I am not ready to agree
- I want more information
- I want to speak to someone else.

*S*eek solution-based responses: "What if this fails to work for you?" "What do you require to ensure that it works?" "It appears like there's something that disturbs you."

*T*here are 2 categories of yes:

1. Confirmation
2. Counterfeit

A counterfeit "yes" refers to one in which your counterpart prepares to say "no" but also feels "yes" is a great escape or wants to make the conversation flowing so that he or she can get more information.

A confirmation "yes" is normally innocent. It is sometimes used to set a trap, but normally it is a simple affirmation without a promise of action.

*T*he commitment yes is the genuine yes. This represents a true agreement that results in action. The commitment "yes" is what you are after, but the three types look similar, so you need to learn how to identify which one is being applied.

*W*hether you refer to it as a "buy-in" or "engagement" or something different, great negotiators are aware that their task is to gently direct their colleagues to attain their goals on their own.

*A*pplying all your skills to build rapport, connection, and agreement with a colleague is important. However, that connection is useless unless the other party feels that they are equally responsible for developing the link and the new ideas they develop.

*A*lthough the intensity can be different from one person to another, one thing you can be sure of is that everyone you meet on the way is driven by two primal urges: the desire to feel safe and secure and the demand to feel in control. If you fulfill that drive, you are in the door.

*I*f you attempt to sell something, don't begin with, "Can you spare a few minutes to talk?" Instead, you should ask, "Is now a bad time to talk?" That way, you will either receive a "Yes, it is a bad time" accompanied by a great time, or you receive "No, it's ok" and their full attention.

*F*or that reason, "no" has numerous skills.

- "No," it provides a chance for the real issues to be dealt.
- "No" secures people from making a choice and lets them correct ineffective choices.

- "No" slows everything down so that people can easily embrace the decisions and the agreements they make.
- "No" allows people to feel secure, emotionally comfortable, and be in control of their decisions.
- "No" guides the effort of everyone forward.

*A*nother method to push for "no" in a negotiation is to request the other party what they don't like.

*I*f you put in all your efforts, and still the other party doesn't say "no," you are negotiating with someone who is indecisive or who has a hidden agenda.

*S*aying "no" causes the speaker to feel secure and in control, so you need to trigger it. That is the reason why "is now a bad time to talk?" better than "Can you spare some minutes to talk?"

*S*ometimes, the only option to let your counterpart listen and interact with you is to force them into a "No." That means intentionally mislabeling one of their emotions or asking a ridiculous question.

In case a prospective business partner ignores you, get in touch with a clear and short "No"-oriented question that implies you are ready to walk away.

. . .

"*H*ave you given up on the following project?" does wonders.

GET THEM TO AGREE TO SMALL THINGS FIRST

Before you persuade your counterpart to come and see what you are trying to achieve, you have to say the things that will let them say, "That's right."

"*T*hat's right" is far better than "yes." Seek for it. Attaining "that's right" in a negotiation builds a break-through.

*A*pply a summary to spark a "that's right." The foundation of a great summary is a label combined with paraphras-ing. Select, rearticulate, and emotionally assure "the world according to..."

BEND THEIR REALITY

The most interesting word in negotiations is "Fair."

*A*s a great negotiator, you need to seek a reputation for being fair. Your reputation should precede you. Allow it to precede you in a manner that creates a means for success.

· · ·

*B*e aware of the emotional drivers, and you can channel the benefits of any deal in a language that will synch.

*T*o attain real leverage in a competitive negotiation, you need to persuade the other party that they have something to lose in case the deal falls through.

*T*his is how you can achieve that:

*T*rigger Their Emotions

To change the reality of your counterpart, you have to begin with the basics of empathy. Begin with an accusation audit accepting all of their fears. By triggering their emotions in preparation for a loss, you make the other party be careful and accept any chance to avoid making a loss.

*L*et the Other Person be the First... Most of the Time

Going first is not the best thing in a negotiation. Allow the other side to anchor monetary negotiations. By allowing them to anchor, you may be lucky. You also need to be careful when you let the other party anchor first. You have to get ready physically to persevere the first offer. If your counterpart is a pro, he or she may push for an extreme anchor to change your reality.

. . .

If You Mention Numbers, Highlight Only Odd Ones

Numbers that end with zero appear like temporary placeholders that can easily be deducted. However, anything that doesn't include zero looks like a figure you arrived at after careful consideration.

Surprise With a Gift

You can let your counterpart get into a mood of being generous by placing an extreme anchor, and after the first rejection, provide them with an unrelated surprise gift.

BUILD AN ILLUSION OF CONTROL

When you walk into a store, rather than inform the salesclerk what you require, you can describe what you are looking for and request suggestions. Once you select what you want, rather than hit them with a hard offer, you can tell them that the price is more than what you had budgeted and request help with one of the greatest-of-all-time questions. For example, "How am I supposed to achieve that?"

These questions have the potential to enlighten your counterpart on what the problem is instead of triggering a conflict by telling them what the problem is.

You need to apply these questions as early as possible, and there are some that you will get that you can apply at the start of each conversation. "What is the greatest challenge you experience?" is one of those questions.

*H*ere are some huge standbys that you can use in almost every negotiation, depending on the circumstances:

- How can I assist in making this sound better for both of us?
- What about this is critical to you?
- How would you like me to continue?
- What is it that led us to this instance?
- How can we solve this issue?
- How am I supposed to handle that?

*G*oing for calibrated questions allows your counterpart to think that they are in control, but it is just you who is guiding the conversation.

*E*ven with the right techniques and methods, if you want to come on top, you still need to learn how to control your emotions.

A great technique to make sure your emotional state is relaxed is to bite your tongue.

*W*hen someone abuses you verbally, disarm your counterpart by asking a calibrated question.

. . .

When people think like they are in control, they apply what psychologists refer to as a hostage mentality. This means, in times of conflict, they react to their absence of power by becoming extremely defensive.

Avoid using questions whose response is "yes" or brief information. These need little thought and motivate the human desire for reciprocity. You will need to give something back.

If you use calibrated questions, make sure to start with words such as "what" or "How." By requesting the other party for assistance, these questions will create an illusion of control in your counterpart and motivate them to talk for long, disclosing important details.

However, don't ask questions by applying the "why" unless you want the other party to defend a goal that serves you. In any language, "why" is considered an accusation.

Personalize your questions to direct your counterpart toward solving your issues. This will motivate them to expend their energy on defining a solution.

There is always a team on the opposite side. If you aren't affecting those behind the table, you will be vulnerable.

AFFIRM EXECUTION

Negotiators need to be decisive architects. To attain consent and execution, they need to design, in a dynamic and adaptive way, the verbal and nonverbal aspects of the negotiation.

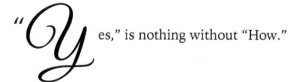

"*Y*es," is nothing without "How."

*A*s long as you have sufficient "How" questions, you can proceed to read and channel the negotiating environment in a manner that you will eventually receive the response you want.

The secret to "How" questions is that they are gentle and graceful means to say "No" and direct your counterpart to build a better solution. A gentle How/No triggers collaboration and leaves your counterpart with a feeling of having been handled with respect.

*A*part from saying "no," the other advantage of asking "How?" is that it causes your counterpart to consider and describe how a deal will be executed.

*B*y letting your counterparts describe the execution in their own words, your "How" questions will persuade them to think like they are defining success in their way: "How can we know that we are on the right track?" and "How will we address things if we discover we are on the wrong track?" When they respond, you summarize their responses until you get a "That's right." Next, you will know they have acknowledged.

*B*e careful of two important signs that your counterpart doesn't believe the idea belongs to them. When they say, "You are right," it is always a great indicator they have not bought into what is being conversed.

*W*hen you request for execution and they reply, "I will try," remember that it implies, "I plan to fail."

*W*hen you listen to either of the above, dive in with calibrated "How" questions until they define the terms of a successful execution using their words.

*F*ollow up by providing a summary of what they have mentioned getting a "That's right."

*Y*ou need to watch out for "Level II" members that are not directly involved but who can assist in completing agreements they like and prevent the ones they don't want.

*H*ere are some tools and techniques for applying subtle verbal and nonverbal types of communication to understand and change the mental state of the other party.

ADDITIONAL TIPS TO HELP THEM SEE YOUR POINT OF VIEW

The Pinocchio Effect

Watch out for the number of times the counterpart uses the phrases I, my, and me. The more times they use these phrases, the less serious they may appear.

7-8-55 Percent Rule

This rule accords 7 percent to the words, 38 percent to the tone of voice of the speaker, and 55 percent to the body language and face.

Study the body language and tone of voice to confirm if they rhyme with the words. If there is a contradiction between the words spoken and the body language, apply labels to ascertain the origin of the difference.

How to Convince Your Counterpart to Compete Against Their Bid?

The right method to make your counterpart to lower their requirements is by saying no using questions. Applying an indirect "no" cannot chase away your counterpart the same way a direct "no" would.

. . .

*S*aying no in a friendly way like, "I'm sorry that doesn't work for me," sounds friendly compared to a direct "no."

*I*f you have no other friendly way of saying no, then "no" is the final and most direct approach. If you say it verbally, then you must try to deliver it using a downward inflection and a tone of regard. It should not be a firm, "NO!"

*A*pply summaries and labels to let your counterpart reaffirm their agreement at least three times. It is quite difficult to fake a conviction.

NEGOTIATE HARD

When you think you are being pushed into a haggle, you can direct the conversation to the non-monetary problems that generate any final price work. You can do this by saying, in a supportive tone of voice, "Let us put aside the price for a moment and discuss what would make this a great deal." Or you could address it directly by asking, "What else can you manage to offer to make that a great price for me?" And in case the other party pushes you to take the mantle, instead of mentioning the price, say a huge number that someone may charge.

*W*hen the negotiation is far from an agreement, you need to trigger things and push your counterpart from their rigid mindset.

. . .

*I*f you want to flip a hesitant counterpart to your direction, you need to ask them, "why would you do that?" but in a manner that the "that" favors you.

*I*f you want to convince a client to migrate from a competitor, you can say, "Why would you ever do business with me?" Why do you want to change from your usual supplier? These are good questions to win a client from a competitor.

*O*nce you have made it clear what your final word is, you need to be ready to walk away. Don't ever be needy for a deal.

SEARCH FOR THE BLACK SWAN

Each case is new. You need to allow what you know to guide you but not blind you.

*A*s a negotiator, you must always be aware of which side, at any time, feels they have the most to lose in case the negotiation fails.

*T*o find leverage, convince your counterpart that they have something real to lose if the deal fails to go through.

. . .

*T*here are three types of leverage: Positive, Negative, and Normative.

*P*ositive leverage describes your potential as a negotiator to offer or withhold things that your counterpart wants.

*N*egative leverage refers to applying the counterpart rules and standards to attain your position. If you can demonstrate inconsistencies between their beliefs and actions, you have normative leverage.

*L*ocating the Black Swans that presents you with a normative valuation can be simple as requesting what your counterpart believes and listening openly. You want to know the type of language they speak and speak it back to them.

*S*ome of the reasons why negotiators may refer to their counterparts as crazy include:

*N*ot Being Informed Properly

People working with incomplete information appear crazy to those with different information.

. . .

*Y*our responsibility when meeting someone like this in a negotiation is to determine what they don't know and deliver that information.

*B*eing Constrained

In any negotiation where your counterpart is behaving in a wobbly manner, there is a possibility that they have things they cannot manage to do, but they don't want to disclose.

*T*hey Have Other Interests

These people are complying with needs and desires that you don't understand based on their set of rules.

*T*he Right Approach to Flush Out Black Swans and Exploit Them

Allow what you know to direct you but not blind you. In any case, you need to remain flexible and adaptable.

*B*lack swans represent leverage multiplies. Don't forget the three types of leverage: positive, negative, and normative.

*W*ork to master the other party's "religion." Diving into worldviews inherently means going past the negotiating table and into the life and emotions of the other party.

MAINTAINING YOUR INVESTMENTS

As a real estate investor, the importance of repairing, maintaining, and managing a real estate property cannot be 0ver stated. Successful real estate investors are known for keeping well managed, removed, and clean investment properties that become an envy of the market. Their meticulous attention and dedication to maintenance are some of the things that give them a tremendous competitive advantage in the market.

If you are looking to become a successful real estate investor, then you need to take property management as a very important part of the game. If you take good care of the property, it will take good care of the tenants, who eventually will take good care of you financially. Not only will your property be fully rented by the right tenants, but it will also increase in value over time.

. . .

*T*his is a secret many mediocre real estate investors fail to learn. They think real estate investing is just about buying and selling properties. It goes beyond that. Property management is what serves the difference between one real estate property and another. This is the reason Alex Delgado said, *"Real estate practice is not about selling or buying a home. It's about representing your client's greatest asset to your client's greatest benefit."*

*W*hat you want to do is to make the property of great value to the client that he/she cannot but to pay the required amount to rent the property. In fact, you can even increase rents when renovations on the underlying property contribute to a high standard of living for tenants. That means more cash flow from the property. When it comes to property management, all it takes is a little creativity and innovation, and you can make your tenants happy.

*U*sually, tenants are happy and proud of their residence when it is highly maintained. They bring their relatives, friends, acquaintances, and business associates to the place because of how superb it is. This provides you with free publicity. Usually, most tenants are more than willing to pay a top dollar when they realize that the tenant is taking good care of the property and making them feel better. This is why you can't take property management for granted if you want to be very successful in real estate investing.

WHY PROPERTY MAINTENANCE?

Property maintenance involves the all-encompassing activity of inspecting, repairing, replacing and renovating a real estate property to ensure that it is kept in good condition and free of any kind of damage that might destroy it. Maintaining real estate is a full-time job that should be done well if you are looking to get the maximum result. The problem with many landlords is that they wait until issues begin to compound before they start dealing with them.

Good property management ensures that you anticipate or inspect the underlying property regularly so that you can resolve issues before they emerge or exacerbate. These days, many tenants have become very keen on the landlord-tenant law, which underlines when and how often a property is supposed to be maintained to meet the rental requirement and be considered safe for the public.

If you don't know how to get a handle on the property maintenance thing, you can simply refer to your local landlord-tenant law and look at what it says about managing and maintaining a real estate property. This will ensure that you maintain the property properly and keep it a good condition for tenants. Always remember that a good property makes happy tenants.

Apart from reading the landlord-tenant law to know how to deal with property management, you can conduct research to learn simple and creative ways to add value to your real estate investment property. Landscaping projects such as creating a garden, a yard, pathway, outdoor section, and painting are all fascinating. Sometimes, only a little renovation is all it takes to give a new facelift to old real estate property. Hence, property management is essential for real estate investing success.

KEY THINGS TO KNOW ABOUT PROPERTY MAINTENANCE

The goal of many real estate investors is to buy a property and bring it to the marketplace and collect rents. While this might seem exciting, many landlords seem to forget and figure out the need for regular property maintenance. Well, the following are some key things about property maintenance you have to keep at the back of your mind when you are considering buying and investing in real estate.

*A*lways Maintain a Standard Building Code

Yes, you want to start collecting rent. But, your tenant wants to ensure that they will enjoy the best possible life when they rent your property. This is why you need to ensure that you maintain a standard building code for all your real estate investment properties. You need to ensure that your properties are fit to a certain level and standard before putting them into the market for rent or sale.

*I*f you fail to deal with critical housing systems such as electricals, plumbing, sewerage, waste management, heating & cooling, a supply of electrical energy, electrical wiring, the flow of water, safety of the electrical appliance, and many others, you'll face a lot of problems with tenants. Tenants don't want to come home and find their possessions on fire because of poor electrical wiring in the house or having no water to shower. Maintain a standard code before putting a property for rent.

Always Factor Unexpected Property Maintenance as Part of the Operating Expense of the Property

It is very important to always budget for property maintenance before it is even needed. Taking good care of your property in real estate investing is not an option; it is a necessity. Many beginner real estate investors are just hoping and praying that their property never has any expenses. While that's good, property maintenance will always come from time to time, and you need to plan towards it.

Not planning for regular and continuous property maintenance is a recipe for disaster. Ideally, consider setting aside at least 10% of monthly rental income towards property maintenance. That does not mean you should blow the money when the property does not really need any maintenance at the moment. But, the essence of it is to ensure that you're proactive with your property maintenance. Budgeting for unexpected and regular expenses keeps you on top of the property maintenance demands of the asset.

Always Be Prompt and Quick in Dealing With Emergency Property Maintenance

Shockingly, some real estate investors seem not to care about emergency maintenance on their property. After they have rented the property, they go to sleep and wake up ready to collect their rents/renewal lease payments. You need to understand that you're in business, and your tenants are your clients.

*F*ailing to promptly deal with emergency property issues exposes the life of the tenants to danger, and you're the one responsible. A breakdown of the housing leading to severe injuries of tenants can cost you a lawsuit and drain your real estate investment capital. This is why it's very important that you are always prompt in dealing with any emergency repair or replacement that a tenant informs you about. This even saves you a lot of dangers when you take care of them quickly. The tenants are in your hands, and you have a responsibility to keep them safe, secure, and sound.

*A*lways Take Care of Turnover Repairs Before Placing the Apartment for Rent

Tenants are required to bear any cost of the damage they have incurred to the property during their stay. Before departing or vacating the rental unit, they are required to ensure that the property has been cleaned and tidied. However, normal wear and tear of the house will require that certain renovations be done before renting the apartment to the next tenant. This is where your responsibility as the landlord comes!

*I*t should start by inspecting the property to look at areas that need some form of work. Consider planning for normal turnover expenses such as painting, landscaping, changing locks, and carpet cleaning of the apartment. Taking care of all these repairs before putting the property on sale will ensure that you get high-quality renters who will be willing to rent the property.

FOUR TYPES OF PROPERTY INSPECTIONS

As a rule of thumb, always schedule a regular inspection code of the property. Inspection is crucial if you want to spot problems before they emerge. You can wait for plumbing problems to start developing before you solve them, or you can schedule regular inspection of your plumbing system to ensure all leaking pipes are handled.

*A*nother typical area that requires regular inspection is roofing. Sometimes, you might not notice that you have a roofing problem until there is rainfall. Leaving leaks in the plumbing system of your toilet undone can cause serious problems for tenants in the house. All these things require regular property inspections to avoid having big problems.

*B*ringing building experts from time-to-time to check on your property is very important. By scheduling a regular inspection, you can catch these small problems and repair them quickly. Failing to do regular plumbing, roofing, drainage, electrical and other forms of inspections can lead to serious damage to your house before you know.

*T*o get started with your property inspections, you need to know and understand the various kinds of inspections undertaken on your property. Just jumping with regular inspection might be good but not very effective in enhancing 100%

maintenance of your property. So, the following are various property inspection types you need to be aware of.

Move-Out Property Inspection

This kind of inspection is very important as it will prepare the rental property for the next tenant. It helps to know the kind of maintenance required to ensure the property is clean, organized, and ready for the next tenant who will be renting it. You get to know the kind of wear and tears that must be done on the property. There are some cases when the current tent needs to be responsible for some repairs due to damages that might have been caused to the property—this kind of inspection helps you to figure this out before the tenant vacates the premises.

Routine Property Inspection

If you want to ensure that your real estate property is always fit, then routine maintenance is a must. You can range quarterly routine-maintenance of the entire property so that you can handle all kinds of issues before they degenerate. Communicating with tenants and discussing with them about possible damages and repairs that needed to be done is a great way to save a lot of hard work.

Move-In Property Inspection

This kind of inspection is very important because it helps the landlord and the tenant to know the state of the property before it was rented. All conditions of the property will be inspected and detailed in the rental lease that will be signed. The landlord expects that the property should be kept in good condition, and there should be no damages except occasional repairs during turnover.

Drive-By Property Inspection

To make sure that your property is in good condition, you can routinely or occasionally check the interior and exterior units of the house to see if everything is in order. You might be able to notice little cracks and leaks that should be handled immediately.

INTERIOR & EXTERIOR UNIT INSPECTION

While there are four types of inspection to be carried about on your real estate investment property, there are two main units that must be inspected. Real estate problems either come from the exterior or the exterior units of the property. When inspecting a property, you want to ensure that all these areas are well checked and issues noted for immediate repairs.

Just like Richard Branson, taking notes of issues he sees in his Virgin Airways, consider your real estate investment as a business. Inspect and take notes of problems you think need to be taken care of and solved well. When you spot a problem with any part of the property or a tenant has informed you, take a look at it and record it in your notebook for repairs.

· · ·

*T*he following are the critical exterior and interior units of the underlying property that needs to be invested each time a real estate inspection exercise is being performed:

*I*nterior Unit Inspection

- Heating & cooling system: Ensure that the filters of the heating and cooling system have been checked regularly to ensure that they are not dirty or inhibited by any foreign material or mold. If the air filter is blocked by any foreign material, it will prevent the free flow of fresh/cool air.

- Interior Painting: You want to ensure that there is no mold growing on the walls and causing the paints to be chipping off the wall. Regularly have the tenants report any incidence of that sort and there get the appropriate experts to repair the interior to ensure everything looks beautiful.

- Smoke detectors: You don't want to live in a room without a smoke detector, do you? No. Neither do your tenants want to live in an apartment where there is no smoke detector? This can be very dangerous and can lead to many unprecedented accidents in the home when an electrical explosion from somewhere emerges.

- Water heater: Checking water heater regularly to ensure that they function well is key to a good interior property inspection. Most people are very attentive to their water heater and don't want to be seeing any dirt from the water because there are all sediments in the water. Focus on working to improve property management systems.

*E*xterior Unit Inspection

- Exterior Painting: Most tenants hate and abhor houses that look dirty and terrible on the outside. They don't feel happy and comfortable. Refusal to paint the exterior of your house when you have to says a lot about you as the tenant. You want to ensure your property reflects your values of neatness and beauty. Ensuring that the exterior of your house is well painted helps to prevent it from being damaged by the sun and moisture.

- The roof: Living in a leaking roof is like living in hell. When it rains, you can't help yourself. If your house has roofing problems, you might want to deal with it and ensure that everything is in good condition before renting. Mold growth, damages, and leaks need to be dealt with for tenants to be safe at night.

- Windows: It's amazing that some rooms don't have windows or they have a poor ventilation system. This tends to drive many tenants away from renting the property. You also want to make sure that the windows of the property are well sealed to avoid during the time of heating and insulation. Old and window repairs need to be taken care of.

- Landscape: A good landscape adds to the aesthetic, beauty, and color of the home. You want to ensure that all trees are well trimmed and those needing cutting are done well. All gardens must be taken care of, and grasses kept green. A well-maintained landscape speaks volumes about the house and the landlord.

DO IT YOURSELF (DIY) & DONE FOR YOU (DFY) PROPERTY MAINTENANCE

Property maintenance is key for a successful real estate investment. Poorly managed and maintained real estate will obviously fail, no matter all the benefits of real estate investors. Therefore, you need to take your property maintenance seriously if you're going to do well. You need to analyze and decide on which approach you want to use to manage the underlying property.

enerally, there are two main options:

. . .

Do it Yourself (DIY) Property Maintenance

As the landlord, you have the responsibility for your house. You can choose to manage all kinds of inspection, repair, and maintenance related to your property. Ideally, this will save your money each month and year. To get the job done, you must leverage the service of other contractors like plumbers, electricians, roofing contractors, painters, and building contractors.

You also need to oversee the work that is done by these professionals to ensure that you get value for your money. Handling all kinds of inspection and maintenance works related to your property takes a lot of time and attention, which can be spent on other real estate investing activities. In addition, you need to make sure you have the right skillset and experience to handle the property management tasks. If you're finding the task challenging, you might want a second option.

Done for You (DFY) Property Maintenance

Property Management companies have the skill, experience, and time to take care of your property. They know how to keep your property well maintained and renovated so that it is sparkling. Many of these firms have years of experience in the field, and their expertise in the field is really breathtaking. When you outsource your maintenance to a credible property management company, you can lessen the burden of running a real estate property.

. . .

*T*hey will save you time and money in the long term and increase the value of your property over time. For a real estate investor who doesn't want to be called at night about fixing toilets and dealing with plumbing work, you can simply outsource the job to a very good property management company that can get the job done. From the exterior to the interior section, the property manager will schedule routine inspections and will do regular maintenance to keep the property in good condition for you.

*Y*ou might, however, be required to pay monthly property management fees. There are some property management companies who even take care of the tenants in the property as well as the property. That means you can scale your real estate investing business. You just have the property management company help rent tenants for you, lease the property, manage the tenant, and keep the property in good condition. The challenge is finding an outstanding property manager with a good track record.

*I*t can be tempting for new real estate investors to want to save money and do the job all by themselves. But the issue is that you can grow a real estate investment empire if you want to be doing all kinds of work related to the property. Leveraging the services of property managers is very important if you want to reduce the workload on you and focus on other things.

PROPERTY MAINTENANCE TIPS

Andrew Syrios, a successful real estate investor, said concerning property maintenance: "Maintenance is the face of your company, and good maintenance is the best form of tenant retention there is. Many tenants are used to poor quality service, so if they come to your place and get good service, it substantially increases the chance that they will want to continue renting from you."

To ensure your tenants are happy, good property maintenance is not optional. The following property maintenance tips will help you as you work on developing and improving your real estate investment property.

1. Be on the lookout for all kinds of leaks, from roofing to plumbing after a severe storm, flooding, and water damage. Arrange with experts to fix these things.
2. Ensure that you have fire extinguishers in the house and they are working well.
3. Regularly fix the heating and cooling systems and replace air filters.
4. All gutters and drainage systems in the house should be clean and tidy.
5. The house should always be clean and neat at all times.
6. Set up a system that ensures that tenants clean the house and keep the property in good shape.
7. All smoke detectors in the house should be checked regularly and fixed.
8. Arrange with a gardener to keep all trees, yards, and flowers in good shape.
9. Ensure that mold and leaks do not develop in the showering system.
10. Pests and insects should be constantly inspected and exterminated from the house.
11. Water heaters should be flushed regularly.

12. All toilets and bathrooms in the house should be kept clean.
13. Sewerage and waste management systems should be handled well.
14. Constantly check locks and safes in the house to ensure they are in good shape.
15. Fence the house to avoid thieves breaking into the house. If possible, set up a security system.

*R*egular property maintenance will not only keep your property in good shape, but it reduces your costs of running the property. It will save you money. Therefore, consider who will take care of the property and get the job done well. As the landlord and the real estate investor, do you have the skills and expertise to provide efficient management for the property? Can you get the job done well? If you can't, simply look for a good property manager and negotiate a good price. Then outsource the management so that you can focus on growing your real estate investment business.

REAL ESTATE INVESTING MISTAKES TO AVOID

TODAY, there are countless blogs, podcasts, YouTube, and TV Programs with many so-called "multi-million real estate investors" who preach that real estate investing is easy and the safest way to create great wealth. Well, while many wealthy people have used real estate investing as a vehicle to build their financial empire, it is important to know that success in real estate doesn't come by chance.

It requires a lot of sacrifices, hard work, focus, and perseverance to succeed. If you're not committed to the game, you're not going to make it. Real estate investing involves dealing with a lot of money, and if you lose focus, you can just sink the financial ship and have a shipwreck. This is why staying objective when it comes to real estate is crucial.

. . .

*U*nfortunately, the problem with many beginner investors is that they think it is so easy. They make the mistake of thinking real estate investing is very cheap and easy, which makes them not give the required attention needed for success. This is one of the things that have crippled many real estate investors. They assume that everything will be cool, and when they face reality, they run into debt and declare bankruptcy.

"*T*he reality is, real estate investing isn't always as rosy or predictable as the TV shows make it out to be. This is true whether you invest in homes to 'flip' them for new buyers, or whether you invest in rental properties to build long-term, passive income," says Holly Johnson.

*R*eal estate investing is not like investing in stocks, bonds, ETFs, and mutual funds. These investment vehicles require less attention and control. After you have invested your money, you don't have to actively manage the investment in order to generate a return. For example, when you invest in a dividend-paying stock, you receive monthly and quarterly payments without doing any work.

*T*his is different when it comes to real estate investing. You have to understand the market and ensure that all the properties are well managed to be profitable in the long term. That's the reason Terrel Gates, a successful real estate investor and portfolio manager, said, "Unfortunately, to be consistently successful in real estate over the long haul requires more skill than luck."

The following are some of the notable mistakes you have to avoid while investing in real estate.

- Not doing a professional inspection before buying
- Not keeping an eye on the numbers
- Not building enough cash reserves
- Not screening tenants before renting
- Not building a team and playing it solo
- Getting bad advice that ruins property
- Investing without a plan
- Lack of proper research
- Recruiting the wrong people
- Possessing a get-rich-quick mentality
- A huge amount of expenditure
- Unplanned expenses
- Not having a backup plan

NOT DOING A PROFESSIONAL INSPECTION BEFORE BUYING

So, you want to save money on a professional inspection. As a result, you did not do good research or professional inspection before buying the property. As a result, you ended up spending a lot of money on renovation and maintenance than you should. This simply leads to high operating costs, which tend to create a lot of problems.

Hiring a professional real estate inspector will help you analyze the status of the property and the estimated amount of money you will spend to renovate it before renting or selling it. Getting a professional home inspector will reveal any hidden cost that you might not see at first. It will also help you avoid buying real estate properties that will become a liability rather than an asset.

*A*void buying real estate properties without doing a professional inspection. Before you make any purchase, check whether the property is worth the price, investing, and managing to generate the estimated returns. If you notice that the property will not help you, just cut your losses and move onto the next property.

NOT KEEPING AN EYE ON THE NUMBERS

If you're not good with accounting, real estate investing can be big trouble for you. When you are using other people's money to invest in real estate, you are accountable. You need to ensure that all funds invested in the property are well managed. And that means keeping regular attention on the numbers of the game.

If you don't keep your books or your books are not well kept, you're not going to make it. You might run into serious losses as a result of poor financial record keeping. To be a professional real estate investor that banks, credit unions, and other investors will trust, you need to maintain clean financial records of your business.

*A*nd you must have your financial team produce weekly, monthly, quarterly, and annual financial reports that will help you keep the focus on building the business. Have a clear idea of your mortgage, tax, operating costs, profit margin, and all others before buying a property. As the rich dad said, "Your profit is made when you buy, not when you sell."

NOT BUILDING ENOUGH CASH RESERVES

In real estate investing, cash is king. After you purchase the real estate, you need cash to maintain and manage the property. If you don't have the required cash to get the whole business going, you can be in trouble. For example, you want to make sure you can set aside for unexpected vacancies before they happen.

*T*his can help you take care of your mortgage and tax payments so that you don't have any problems. You might also decide to plan for unexpected repairs and renovations, which might happen in the process of time. Building a strong cash reserve will help you to weather both the bull and bear market. When the market is tough, your cash reserves can keep you going before everything turns out well.

*S*easoned real estate investors are known to set aside about 10% to 20% of their annual rental income as a reserve to take care of anything that might happen. This cash serves as a cushion to prevent shocks that can damage your real estate empire.

NOT SCREENING TENANTS BEFORE RENTING

In haste to start collecting rents, many real estate investors just go for a bunch of low-quality tenants that give them a lot of headaches. The tenant avoids paying rent, mismanages, and damages the property. They quarrel with their tenants and landlord and make a living in the house unbearable. This kind of tenant must be screened and avoided in the first place.

· · ·

*J*ust because a person has money to rent does not mean you should rent for them. You've got to set a standard and detail the type of tenant you want. When you run your ad, you should make it known to those who show up about your terms and conditions.

*C*heck the credit and criminal history of the tenants before renting your property to them. While you need to screen tenants, you must also avoid any act of discrimination in relation to sex, religion, and race to avoid getting into trouble with the Federal Housing Administration (FHA).

NOT BUILDING A TEAM AND PLAYING IT SOLO

As said earlier about building your real estate empire, you need a team. Even if you don't want to build a real estate empire, you can't handle multiple real estate properties alone. Trying to save money by playing it solo will kill you. The stress and pressure of managing a rental real estate property are much more than one person can do.

*K*elvin Ortner said, "Owning a commercial or residential rental property can be both time- and capital-intensive. Trying to handle it all solo can require a level of focus and commitment that may not be realistic for every investor. A simple way to avoid that mistake is building a team from day one." Leverage a team to manage the property to avoid bearing all the stress alone. Don't make this mistake.

NOT KNOWING AND UNDERSTANDING THE MARKET

You have to understand your market before you purchase real estate. This is true whether you are buying to rent or buying to sell. As a real estate investor, you don't make a profit by just holding the property. That's appreciation. However, the profit is made when you rent or sell the property. As a result, you need to understand the dynamics of the buying and selling market before you buy.

*B*uying real estate in an area where jobs are moving is a recipe for disaster. You are just going to lose money. That's the reason you have to listen to local, national, and international news before buying any real estate investment. If the government is going to demolish buildings in an area and you went ahead to buy a property there, you'll be in trouble.

*P*ay close attention to the market and get accurate information about the area before investing. An entrepreneur will do market research to know and understand his customer before producing a product. This increases the prospects of success. You need to do the same thing. Have a good understanding of the rental and tenant condition of the area before investing.

GETTING BAD ADVICE THAT RUINS THE PROPERTY

Nothing kills real estate like bad advice. Therefore, you need to be careful about the kind of advice you take in running your real estate properties. You have to learn to take advice but carefully analyze them before acting on them. Listen to people, but follow your own judgment, decisions, and intuition. Don't just do something because someone told you to do it.

 $\mathcal{T}$ he biggest mistake many real estate investors make is listening to their real estate broker or agent too much. They fail to do their own research and, out of greed, invests in a losing property that drains their cash flow and capital. Don't let this happen to you. Always make sure you have questioned, reviewed, and evaluated any advice carefully before taking action.

INVESTING WITHOUT A PLAN

If you are planning to invest in real estate, the most important thing for you is to have a plan. Investing in real estate can get costly, and investing impulsively is not a good idea. If you don't do proper research and planning before making your investment, you may end up paying a lot more than you anticipated. Before investing, you need to look at the potential of the property, its present market value, how much work needs to be done on it, the maintenance cost, etc.

LACK OF PROPER RESEARCH

Selling and owning properties involves many nuances. The property may require certain permits, and you may need to be aware of the zoning laws as well. If the property is located in some area prone to natural disasters, then it will have an impact on how much you spend on the insurance. You need to research whether the property has some kind of insect damage or whether or not someone died an unnatural death in that property. If you find these kinds of issues, you may consider making necessary changes in the price of the property.

RECRUITING THE WRONG PEOPLE

If you are investing in real estate, you are likely to use it for growing your retirement fund. In this case, your self-directed individual retirement account (SDIRA) owns that property. It simply means that you will not be able to work on it. However, you can choose who can work on it. This is quite dangerous because you can lose a lot of money if you end up hiring the wrong people. You may end up overpaying them. So, it is very necessary that you do your research about the property as well as about the people you hire.

POSSESSING A GET-RICH-QUICK MENTALITY

There is a common misbelief that you can be instantly wealthy by investing in real estate. Well, that is not quite true. It is a long-term investment. It takes your money as well as your patience and time. It can give you fruitful results if you make the right moves at the right times. The property is not liquid. So, it is quite difficult to unload it when you are already losing money on it. You may find yourself holding onto a property for quite a long time. So, make sure that you have patience and determination.

A HUGE AMOUNT OF EXPENDITURE

The biggest mistake that you can make while investing in real estate is when you spend a lot of money on your investment. Be aware that you don't get stuck in a money pit. If you are considering renting your property, make sure that it isn't vacant for too long. The more it stays vacant, the more it is going to cost you. It can even cost you if you rent your property to the wrong people. So, if you want to avoid huge unnecessary expenses, choose your property carefully and also the people you want to rent it to.

UNPLANNED EXPENSES

The most important thing that you need to keep in your mind while investing in real estate is the fact that it is not cheap. The one responsible for funding the upkeep of your real estate is your IRA. All the little costs, i.e., the gas bill, electricity bill, etc., add up. As mentioned earlier, investing in real estate is a long term business, so if you jump in without a proper expense plan, then you may end up suffering huge losses in the long run.

NOT HAVING A BACKUP PLAN

Having a plan b must be a part of your plan. It is obvious that you want success in your real estate investment, but sometimes you may find yourself sitting on it for way too long. For benefitting your IRA, you may need to make certain modifications in your plan. There are chances that you may not have to use your exit strategy at all. But, you still need to have it in case you do. So, before making an investment in real estate, make sure that you are ready to face every kind of situation that may arise in the future.

CONCLUSION

Thank you for making it through to the end of *The Automatic Millionaire*; let's hope it was informative and able to provide you with all of the tools you need to achieve your goals, whatever they may be.

I wrote this book with the idea in mind that I want to help others achieve their own investment goals and retire early without having a single worry in the world. I hope this book was able to achieve that goal. This book was not only aimed at teaching you the intricacies of buying and selling but also the different nuances of strategic planning that differentiates an expert from a beginner.

By now, you must have understood that there is a reason that everyone flocks to real estate – you can really make a handsome amount of money, and it is also one of the fastest ways to gain financial freedom. But there is no secret strategy in the world that is going to make all of that happen overnight. You need time and patience and also strategize properly.

CONCLUSION

I hope you were able to learn many new things from this book, but now, it is time for you to apply them in real life.

HOW TO TURN YOUR SIDE HUSTLE INTO A
PASSIVE INCOME SOURCE

Retire Early

NATHIN O'BRIEN

INTRODUCTION

Welcome, and thank you for choosing this book! Within these pages, you will find a wealth of information to get you ready for your perfect passive income business.

WHO IS THIS BOOK FOR?

There are many different side hustles; you can either build your own business or work on a freelance, contract, or on-call for another company. If you want to find a way to make an income while you sleep or while working your day job, this book is for you!

WHAT BENEFITS WILL YOU GAIN FROM READING THIS BOOK?

In this book, we will be learning about side hustles' characteristics. We will spend the majority of our time focusing on one specific type; passive income streams that you can work on without much effort on your part.

Throughout this book, you will be provided with plenty of examples of different types of side hustles and business ideas for passive income. This information will help you understand the difference between a part-time job and a legitimate side hustle and will help you begin making passive income for yourself!

This book aims to help you create a side hustle for yourself and turn it into a passive income source. You can eventually make enough money to make large, secure investments like purchasing a house or investing in stocks! Continue reading if you want to find freedom from your day job and develop a passive income source for yourself. It's never too late to begin saving for retirement or your next vacation! It's never too late to get out of debt once and for all!

WHAT IS PASSIVE INCOME?

WE WILL BEGIN the book by defining several terms so that you can continue reading the following chapters with confidence! This chapter will teach you what a side hustle is and the income you can gain.

WHAT IS PASSIVE INCOME?

Before we dive into the rest of this book, wherein we will discuss specific examples of passive income sources that you can benefit from, I want to give you an overview of the topics you will be learning. I will begin by defining *passive income* for you.

Passive income is a type of income that derives from a business or enterprise where the person is not actively involved. Passive income is different from the types of jobs people usually spend their time doing because passive income does not require nearly as many hours of work as your regular jobs do. Below, we will look at some of the differences between active and passive income.

THE DIFFERENCE BETWEEN PASSIVE INCOME AND ACTIVE INCOME

Now you might be wondering why it matters if which type of income you make when they both produce money for you in the end? Well, it matters because your ability to accomplish your financial goals depends on you understanding these two different terms. Below, I have defined both of them for you.

- Active Income

Active income means that the income you receive is for a series of services that you have performed. Examples of active income include; salaries, wages, commissions, tips, and business endeavors. Examples of this would be someone working as a teller at the bank. They get paid in salary, and they are getting paid in exchange for the services they perform for one specific company. Another example would be a waiter working at a restaurant; the wages they earn per hour are their active income, so are the tips they make. They actively perform services for one specific establishment and are an employee of the business.

- Passive Income

As I mentioned, passive income is a type of income that derives from a business or enterprise where the person is not actively involved. Passive income may include income from a rental property, a company they share in, or renting out their car on share websites.

- Active Income Versus Passive Income

*I*n the simplest terms, active income means that you are physically doing something to obtain income, whereas passive income means you are 100% hands-off or close to it.

MORE ON PASSIVE INCOME

If you want to make enough money to live on and save for a comfortable retirement, passive income may not be enough. However, you could create a situation for yourself where you have two different types of income working together to speed up the process of achieving your goal. This point brings us to the term *Side Hustle*.

WHAT IS A SIDE HUSTLE?

A side hustle is almost like a 'second-job' that provides you with another source of income. Rather than being employed by someone else or another company, a side hustle is a business that you opened yourself 'on the side' that is either your passion project or another method to help make you money.

SIDE HUSTLE VS. A SECOND JOB

Side hustles are not the same as a second job or a part-time job. Your employer will be managing your time and how much pay you receive for that time at a part-time job. On the other hand, side hustles give you the freedom to decide how much you want to earn and how many hours you want to work.

With financial security becoming a considerable problem for nearly 50% of Americans, side hustles have become a popular option for people looking to get out of debt or are just interested in starting their own business.

HOW DOES A SIDE HUSTLE WORK?

You will work to build your side hustle during the hours outside of your day job. Due to this, your working hours for your side hustle will likely take place during weekends, evenings, or holidays.

If you have goals that require a lot of money, then creating multiple sources of passive income on top of your active income may be the ideal route. However, if your goals do not require large sums of money, then maybe you can even comfortably live off of one source of passive income, or no passive income at all, just active income.

WHAT IS FINANCIAL FREEDOM?

Overall, people consider side hustles to achieve *financial freedom*. Financial freedom means that you no longer have to work to make money actively.

When a person is financially free, it usually means that they no longer have to stress or worry about money. Becoming financially free may sound simple, but this differs significantly in different people. Some people may define themselves as financially free if they have enough income coming into support for their traveling, partying, and fancy vacations. To other people, financial freedom may simply mean that they don't have to worry about paying rent or their electric bills anymore.

HOW TO TURN YOUR SIDE HUSTLE INTO A PASSIVE INCOME SOURCE

It is important to note that you should not be confused with a side hustle being a full-blown, standalone business. Most people who start their side hustle still have to work a traditional full-time job simultaneously. The reason for this is because side hustles may not generate enough (or any) income until you get the proper traction and marketing to begin making money. Having a full-time job enables you to have the ability to pay your bills while also spending some of your free time building your side-hustle, so eventually, it does start creating a separate stream of income.

In the beginning, you will have two sources of active income, one is your day job, and the second being the income that you make from your side hustle business. However, you could turn your side hustle business into a passive income source if you can grow it to the point where you can employ other people to work for your business or offer services to your business. At that point, you can hire somebody else to manage your business functions, such as accounting and operations, and you can sit back and just collect the money as it comes in. At this point, it will become a passive income source for you.

Getting to the point of gaining passive income does take quite a bit of time, work, dedication, and luck. Still, if you want to develop a sustainable source of passive income without many resources, you will have to grow your side hustle until it is big enough to become a standalone business. At that point, it can begin to provide you with passive income.

Starting a side hustle business is a great way for you to start saving some extra money. This extra money will open up two options for you:

*T*he first option is to grow your coaching business into one that is big enough that it turns into a good stream of passive income.

*T*he second option is to grow your side hustle business into big enough where you can employ or contract other people to do the groundwork for you. What this means is that you will aim to reach a point when your side hustle business develops a reputation that is good enough for you to have a steady stream of business (or too much business for you to handle alone). At that point, you can begin hiring employees or contractors to work for your business. Hiring people is a good way to turn your side hustle business into a passive income source. If done properly, you would be able to hire someone to manage your operations and a team of people that work with your clients while you sit back and enjoy the flow of revenue.

One thing to keep in mind is that in between, as you grow your business, there may be a period where this becomes an active income source. There may come the point while growing your side hustle business when its income begins to exceed your current active income (your day job). At this point, you can comfortably replace your day job with your side hustle (aka your side hustle becomes your day job). However, this would mean that your coaching business will not become a stream of passive income. If, though, you choose the second option instead, you can hire others to run your business while you continue your day job.

You ideally want to upgrade your passive income as you earn more money to eventually achieve one or several short-term goals that will help you meet your specific financial freedom goals in the future. Regardless of which option you choose, one of your interim goals should be to save up the money you make from your side-hustle to eventually build a strong stream of passive income. One example of a strong investment is investing in a property, for example, as this is one of the most secure and reliable investments to make. This investment can also help you develop even more passive income by doubling it as a rental property. In my opinion, the best type of passive income is some type of investment, whether it's in stocks, bonds, or property. We will discuss this further in this book, but guaranteed income (like an investment property) is the way to go if you are not risk-averse and just want to increase your overall income.

AN IMPORTANT NOTE ABOUT LONG-TERM PASSIVE INCOME

I want you to remember that keeping money in a savings account that does not generate you any money means losing money. Inflation is set at approximately 2% per year, so if you are not investing every dollar in your savings account, you lose 2% of your savings every year. As much as I will be focusing on building side hustles and passive income streams in this book, I want to make sure that you are also making a plan for investing the money you will make from these side hustles. These investments could be in a property, some stocks, or even just a high-interest savings account. Make sure you are doing that along the way.

HOW TO CHOOSE A SOURCE OF PASSIVE INCOME

IF YOU ARE READING this book, you are likely someone who is ambitious and is looking to create more income to achieve the specific goals that will give you financial freedom in the future. So, let's talk a little more about how you can determine what you want your side hustle to be.

Did you know that the average household in America has about $15,000 in credit card debt? Thanks to the spending culture that the Western world has fostered, people tend to spend money that they don't have through the use of credit cards and loans. Side hustles are a great way to make extra money to pay off existing debt and to begin building a savings account that you can use to generate more money in the future. If you can accomplish these goals with passive income, that is even better!

There are many different side hustles to choose from; you can either build your own business or work on a freelance, contract, or on-call basis for another company. Some of these options are better suited to become passive income sources down the line, and we will discuss this throughout the chapters in this book. Again, keep in mind that a side hustle is different than a part-time job- as being employed as an "employee" simply means that you now have two jobs. However, picking up contracts or freelance work is a side-hustle because you get to choose how much you want to work and when you do it.

Later in this book, you will be provided with more examples of different side hustle options and businesses – this will help you understand the difference between a part-time job and a legitimate side hustle. The chapters that follow will also give you some ideas for your side hustle. Keep in mind that your side hustle's goal is to create a source of passive income for yourself as you read through this chapter.

EXAMINE YOUR RESOURCES

The first step in choosing a passive income source is to examine the resources you have access to.

It is essential to talk about your current resources and examine whether you have enough of these resources to support your perfect side hustle. For instance, if you are interested in starting a business, it will not provide you with passive income at first, so you must make sure you have a secure day job that can support you while you get your side hustle going.

. . .

Financial Resources

Now, if you have many resources to work with, there are much easier ways to generate passive income without starting a business first. Have you ever heard the saying, "your first million is the hardest?" this is because money begins to make itself when you have enough of it. For this type of person, you will be more interested in the financial realm of passive income, such as Stocks, Bonds, Commodities, and so on. We will discuss this in chapter four, but for now, keep in mind that you can essentially start making passive income immediately if you have a lump sum of money.

For instance, if you have a small fortune saved up, think like $20,000. You can easily put that $20,000 into high-interest savings account at your local bank and generate 2-3% interest on it monthly. Doing this means that you are making $4,800 - $7,200 yearly by doing nothing at all. Although breaking it down into a monthly income, it's not much. That being said, simply just putting your money in a high-interest savings account can make you as much as any other new side hustle can. This method is the easiest way to make a passive income, but you could make even more money by doing other things that are more elaborate. We will look at several examples in chapter four, such as buying a rental property or a car to rent out.

That being said, I understand that most people don't have $50,000 lying around to use as a down payment for a home, so I will spend most of this book talking about building a side hustle or a business that makes sense for you.

Physical Resources

The side gigs in this book will vary in terms of their individual start-up costs. Some may require you to invest in equipment or tools, while others only require your body! Depending on your resources, you may qualify for more or fewer of these options.

For example, are you able-bodied? Do you have some physical resources available already, like a video camera, a car, a second property, a computer, or equipment to run a business of your choice? These resources will influence your choices for starting a side hustle. Moreover, depending on your resources, it will open up doors for your side gig options. For instance, if you have a car, you will qualify to do numerous side gigs requiring a vehicle. If you have a spare house or property, this opens up multiple options for you as well. However, if you are someone with very limited resources, you may have to stick to the side gigs that don't require much equipment.

EXAMINE YOUR SKILLS

The second step to choosing a side hustle or a passive income source is to examine your skills.

Use Your Skills

If you have the skill to start a side business, this will provide you with a higher earning potential than a side hustle that does not require any specific skills. It is beneficial to consider that option first when choosing a side hustle, as it is more suitable for your knowledge, skills, and income.

For instance, many different side hustles out there, ranging from blog platforms to teaching personal training. These side hustles require specific skills and have the potential to earn you an extra income of $500 - $4000 per month.

Use Side Hustle Matching Platforms

Some businesses have created numerous platforms aimed at matching people with specific side hustles based on work skills in our modern world. Thanks to these platforms, about 10% of people have a side hustle in American households today.

OTHER TIPS

I want to note that to find success in your side gigs, don't silo yourself into just one type. You should always have at least two side gigs ongoing so that if one gig is slow in business, you could tap into your other gig more. Having only one side gig puts you at the risk of not being able to pay your bills if it's slow in business for one month. Throughout this book, as I describe what each side gig is and its earning potential, I will also note to describe what type of person this side gig is most suitable for. This information will help you decide on whether or not this side gig is ideal for you. In the scenario that you have started a side gig that you don't enjoy or doesn't meet the earning potential you imagined, then I encourage you to try a few others. Finding the perfect side gig that you enjoy, pays well, and allows you to balance your time as a musician takes trial and error. Don't give up just because the first side gig you tried didn't meet your expectations, try something else, and keep at it until you find one that works for you.

The final factor to note is that we have to keep in mind that the different side gigs featured in this book vary in popularity and earning potential depending on where you are located in the world. For instance, San Francisco will have many side gigs due to the high-tech and populated city compared to rural areas with a low population. If you are located in a big city, then luck is on your side. Most of these side gig suggestions will apply to you and will likely have a large client base. However, if you live in rural North Dakota, some of these side gigs will not make sense.

In the next chapter, we will be talking about all the different types of passive income sources out there, and you will have a better idea of which one suits you best.

PASSIVE INCOME IDEAS- ONLINE

IN THIS CHAPTER, we will look at ways to create a side gig for yourself online! Online side gigs often involve creating content for people to enjoy. This content can include videos, pictures, or anything you can show on the internet to curious viewers and scrollers. There is a large market for content creation today since the internet and social media have such a massive presence in our society.

If you can take advantage of this, you can provide yourself with an income source by merely posting content on the internet. Once you develop a following for yourself, you can begin to make money by giving this following with pictures and videos of yourself. You will get paid through advertising and views, which is an excellent way to make passive income.

We will begin by looking at the different options you have to put your content up for everyone to see.

ADVERTISING INCOME ON VIDEOS

There are many different platforms where you can post your videos to have them make money. Each of these platforms is a little different, and I will explain each of them below.

YOUTUBE

The first platform is YouTube. Everyone is aware of YouTube's existence, but not everyone knows how to use it to make money. If you have a large following on YouTube, companies will take note of this. Once they notice your following, they will choose one of two ways to use your channel for advertising;

1. They will sponsor your videos by having you mention their name and the products or services they offer.
2. They will pay to have ads placed at the beginning of (or partway through) your videos to attract customers to their brand.

Either of these two ways that businesses can advertise to your following can bring you monthly income. YouTube provides the creators with 55% of the revenue from ads earned on a video.

There are several ways that you can create videos to get a high number of views and eventually advertising on those videos. This section will explore some of these video themes that are popular today on video hosting platforms.

Mukbang

The first video theme is called Mukbang. Mukbang is pronounced as *"Muk-bang"* and is a Korean word that loosely means "let's eat broadcast." This type of video involves eating large amounts of food in front of the camera.

People will often eat Korean foods like kimchi or spicy instant noodles, and sometimes people will dip foods in cheese sauce before eating it. In these videos, people eat regularly so that the videos can last for some time. It began as a Korean trend, but now some people will film a Mukbang video eating food. If you like to eat and you are comfortable enough to do this in front of the camera, you may want to consider filming one of these popular types of videos for YouTube. Some people film Mukbang videos, which have become quite famous, and can make themselves a hefty sum of money by merely eating on camera.

Critiques

Another popular type of video that people can make for YouTube is critique videos. These videos can be critiques of anything, so you can choose something about which you are passionate. Some common types of critiques include music video critiques, award show critiques, red carpet critiques, critiques of other YouTube videos, and movie and TV show critiques. You can speak to the camera stating your opinions while including clips of the video or show that you are critiquing and let your personality show through, as this is what gets people interested in your content.

Web series

A web series is a recurring set of videos that you post to the internet on a video hosting site like Vimeo, YouTube, or Facebook Watch. This set of videos can be scripted or unscripted and can be about any topic. For example, you could write a scripted series about a musician trying to make it big or an unscripted behind-the-scenes look at a musician's life. If your series gets enough views, you will continue making money on your videos as people will eventually look forward to their release dates (for example, every Tuesday). Setting regular release dates will give your videos guaranteed views, which will motivate you to keep making them. If you already have a following, this is a great option, but it is also a good option for people looking to develop a following. If you attract people with your web series, they will likely subscribe and browse your channel's rest to see what other videos you have posted.

Others

There are even more options, depending on your skills and experiences. For example, if you are a musician, you probably have many topics you could make videos about, such as informative videos on how to string a guitar or play a specific song on the drums. Making something you are passionate about will show through in your energy on camera, so choosing something that you care about and are also knowledgeable about will help you to create good quality videos that people will like. You can make videos on literally anything, so play around a bit and see what you enjoy making. If you enjoy it, chances are other people will as well.

VIMEO

Vimeo is another video hosting site, but this one usually contains videos made more of an art form. Budding filmmakers or musicians can post their music videos on Vimeo, which is more suited to a higher level of video production quality.

If you already have a following, you can choose to sell your videos to your fans for a price that you can set. You can make income for yourself through your videos, and your followers can support your work in this way.

There is also some advertising income that you can make through Vimeo, but to a lesser extent than on YouTube. Since this platform aims to showcase high-quality videos, some people feel that they would be "tarnished" by the presence of ads, as it states directly on the Vimeo website.

CONTENT WRITING

When it comes to side gigs in content creation, content writing is a great choice. The platforms within this category are specialized within the business writing industry. This industry includes company blogs, LinkedIn articles, and specific niche blogs. If you are a creative person, you may not be a stranger to writing music or words, and you may have the necessary transferrable skills to be successful at it. In terms of flexibility, freelance writing is extremely flexible since you can do it anywhere and anytime.

The earning potential is fairly high, depending on what sorts of work you are qualified to write and how quickly you can write. The faster you can write, the more money you can make on an hourly basis. There are a few platforms that help connect content writers to businesses and people that require this talent. We will look at a couple of examples below, including *Problogger, medium, LinkedIn,* and self-publishing books or articles are methods where you can create income. Let's take a look at each of these platforms and methods and how you can utilize them to make money.

Problogger

Problogger is a platform where it connects business-owners or individuals who require blogs written for their business to people who have experience doing blog-writing. Problogger offers services for starting a blog and creating content.

The earning potential through this platform varies widely depending on the business demand. Most bloggers can make over $100 per month, but that's pretty low compared to other side gigs you can do to generate more income. The benefit is that you can write a blog anytime, anywhere- as long as you reach the deadline required by the client. New projects and blog requests are posted each day for people to pick up as needed.

One drawback is that you may have to spend time sifting through the projects and figuring out which ones you are best qualified for.

ADVERTISING INCOME ON BLOGS

If writing is something of interest to you, you may make more money writing e-books and articles for larger companies than writing your blog as their workflow is more consistent, and the rates are much higher. That being said, if you can gain a significant following, you can make advertising money passively from your blog. If this is the direction you would prefer to go, you must understand that it will take time and energy to build up the fanbase needed to begin earning income from your blog. Below we will look at some examples of ways to make advertising income from your blog.

USING A BLOG WRITING PLATFORM

- Medium.com

Medium.com is a platform full of blogs and articles are written by amateurs and professionals for avid readers to study their content. You can also write for medium.com to generate some income but bear in mind that this stream of income varies widely and is lower than other side gigs. It has high flexibility as you can essentially write about whatever you want, whenever you want, and get paid every month. If you have experience or a particular interest in writing content of all styles and topics, this may be a side gig that is right for you!

STARTING YOUR OWN CONTENT WRITING BUSINESS

Another way to generate income from writing is to start your own independent writing side gig. This method is more elaborate than utilizing platforms to connect you to clients as it requires you to find your clients and pitch your skills based on your needs. You can do this by developing a strong sales pitch that consists of your experience, writing skills, and why you are a good option for a business to hire you. Businesses tend to look for people who can write articles, books, and white papers.

There is a TON of undiscovered business in this area, and all it takes to tap into a steady and high source of side gig income is finding the right client who trusts in your skills.

One method to approach finding clients is looking for Content Managers or businesses on LinkedIn and reaching out to them. Try to choose businesses that you know require writers.

To generate business, it is a numbers game. The more people you reach out to with your services, the more likely you will get a hit. Do this at least 100 times a day with different businesses and positions of people; you will likely get some hits back to learn more about what you can offer. The best part about this method is that it has high earning potential if you can find yourself a handful of steady clients. However, if luck isn't on your side, this is not a steady income source as you have to spend hours reaching out to people and pitching your services, and you could end up not having much return on it. This method's flexibility is very high; as I said, you can write anywhere and anytime. The hardest part about making this side gig method work is getting the clients to begin with.

E-BOOK WRITING

One great way to benefit from content writing in a passive form is by writing pieces and uploading them to various locations, which will earn you money. For example, if you write an e-book, you can sell it on amazon or other e-book hosting locations. This way, your book will make money each time someone buys it, and this provides you with passive income.

CREATING YOUR OWN BLOG

Overall, there are numerous ways that you can make money in the realm of content creation. Content creation includes creating unique videos, audio, social media trends, and writing pieces on something called a blog.

These side gigs require some time to ramp up as they are highly dependent on how well your content does in the marketplace. However, the profit generated from this type of work can be extremely high (we're talking over thousands per month) and therefore, people who have talent and skill in this area may be interested in this type of work.

You can always do content creation as one of your income sources and have steadier sources that generate your income while ramping up your content. This way, you are not going without making any money, but you are still allowing yourself to generate income through creating content.

ADVERTISING INCOME ON SOCIAL MEDIA

Social media is a relatively new way to make money since it used to be used solely to connect with friends. Still, now every business has multiple social media accounts- one on every platform. Businesses and brands use these social media accounts to reach consumers and advertise their products. These days, there are advertisements on social media news feeds so that people see them as they are scrolling through their timeline, looking at the people they follow and product placement in people with many followers like celebrities or models.

There are several social media platforms, including Instagram, Facebook, Twitter, Twitch, Tumblr, TikTok, etc. All of these platforms have the potential to make you money if you have a large following, which results in lots of likes on your content or millions of views on your videos. The best way to maximize your following is to cross over your social media accounts, advertising one platform on the other, so that your followers can follow you on every platform possible.

With social media, the earning potential is pretty much unlimited, though you have to reach the social media celebrity level to begin earning a lot of money. If you have around 10 thousand followers, you can begin to get partnerships with brands that will give you free merchandise or up to $150. The money begins to flow when your social media following reaches one million followers. Then, you can begin to make 15 thousand US dollars for a single post! Any number of followers in between will give you some money between $150 and $15 000. A big range, I know. But it depends on the number of partnerships you have and the brands which are paying you to advertise their product for them.

In addition to having many likes and views, there is another way you can make money using social media. You can make money using social media with the help of something called *Social Media Management*. Social media management is when you manage your social media accounts and organize what you will post to maximize your potential reach and visibility. This tool will help you to make the most of your social media reach and make as much as you can use your social media platforms by managing them all from one place.

Hootsuite

Hootsuite is a social media management tool that you can use to manage all of your social media accounts on a single screen. You can include your Facebook, LinkedIn, Twitter, Instagram, and YouTube accounts and keep up with them from one place. In addition to monitoring your likes and views, Hootsuite allows you to schedule your posts so that you can keep your accounts active throughout the day while you are busy or while you are on vacation away from your computer. Hootsuite also allows you to keep track of your reach and the attention your posts get and graph them so that you can compare your results over time.

There is a single place where you can view your comments, your mentions, and where you were tagged and reply straight from the Hootsuite interface. You will also receive notifications from all connected social media accounts so you can keep on top of what is going on in each of them without becoming overwhelmed by having to flip back and forth between apps on your phone.

Hootsuite works on a membership basis, so you must pay a monthly fee if you wish to use their services. This fee and more can be returned to you, however, with the money you have made on your social media platforms as they grow in popularity.

SproutSocial

Another social media management tool is SproutSocial. This social media management platform is similar to Hootsuite in that it allows you to have all of your social media accounts in one place. SproutSocial has different tabs within its home page for different aspects of your social media management. It contains a tab for Publishing, where you can control your posts and schedule them, a tab for Analytics where you can track your activity, and a tab for Engagement to monitor your comments and respond to them straight from the SproutSocial page. With SproutSocial, you can link your Facebook, Twitter, LinkedIn, Instagram, TripAdvisor, and Pinterest too.

ADVERTISING INCOME ON PODCASTS OR RADIO

You can also earn money by creating content by forgetting the video part and producing solely audio content instead. There are different ways to do this, but the most popular and effective way is by making a podcast.

A podcast is a series of audio episodes usually around a specific topic that you can upload to the internet so that your subscribers or listeners can download them. A podcast is usually somewhere between twenty and forty-five minutes in length. Podcasts are often subscribed to on platforms like Apple Podcast, Spotify, or websites and are generally automatically downloaded to subscribers' mobile devices when a new episode is uploaded.

Since podcasts have become so popular in recent years, there is a large market for advertising on them, and many popular podcasters have advertisements at the beginning of their podcasts. Your podcast must have lots of traffic and many subscribers to get advertisements. Further, having your listeners rate your podcast is another way to get noticed by advertisers and listeners.

Podcasts can be about any topic under the sun, from music to news to relationships. Having many personalities and a nice-sounding voice is key to having a good podcast and engaging content from week to week. If you choose a topic you are passionate about, you will never run out of things to discuss. Below are a few examples of themes that you can use for your podcast topic. Your podcast should follow the same general theme, but your episode topics can vary within this.

News

News is a common topic for a podcast. This new theme can focus on a specific type of news like European news, Fishing news, or Technology news. Within this theme, you can choose specific weekly topics depending on what is going on in the world or within the world you chose. Keep people interested by choosing exciting and engaging topics that they will be sure to tune in for. Since you are a musician, you can keep this relevant to music since you can speak well. For example, you can make your podcast theme something like "Indie Music Updates," Each week, choose ten or so updates to include in your podcast to keep people informed in the indie music scene.

Entertainment

This theme is one that you will likely identify with, as you are a musician. Entertainment is quite a broad theme as it can include movies, television, music, and anything that concerns pop culture. In terms of music, you could talk about a specific music genre, about concerts and shows going on in particular cities, or about record labels. The range of topics within entertainment is quite broad, and you will surely be able to find something within this topic that suits your interests and passions.

Educational

Another excellent podcast genre is an *educational* topic. Many people enjoy listening to instructions to learn something instead of reading an instruction booklet or a manual. You can instruct people on how to speak a language, date or conduct themselves in relationships, or any other type of self-help podcast or teach people about music-related topics like how to start a band, write music, or gain a fan base. The possibilities here are endless since you can have a broad theme and continue teaching people new topics each week. If your topic is "How to start a band," you can have a new episode each week on issues like "how to audition new members" and "how to book your first gig."

E-COMMERCE

Let's start by learning a little about online stores, how they can be side gigs, and some of their benefits. Online stores are similar to popular e-platforms like Amazon and eBay. However, the ones that can be utilized as side-gigs are typically on a smaller scale where sellers can post items they've made or second-hand items up for sale. There are numerous amounts of online store platforms that are extremely user-friendly and can help you make money by selling your old items or hand-made items.

The first benefit that comes with using online stores as your side gig is time. You don't have to invest a lot of time into it; all you need to do to get started on most of these platforms are the following:

1. Simply make an account
2. Begin with a few items that you'd like to sell
3. Make a post
4. Reply to the interested people

Yes, it's that simple. However, you have to keep in mind that some items receive more attention from customers than others. For instance, Apple products or any type of decently new electronics tend to get a lot of online attention. These products do well on second-hand online platforms like Letgo, Craigslist, and eBay. If you are artistically skilled and can make homemade crafts like jewelry, pottery (mugs, vases, bowls), knits, etc., you can utilize more specialized websites like Etsy. Let's dive into the different ways that you can begin to make money using online stores.

E-Commerce: Dropshipping

Dropshipping is a fairly new business model that people can use to run their online stores. Dropshipping is simple; essentially, you have your online store with items of your choice to sell. You also have a relationship with a wholesaler that can sell your products at wholesale prices.

You could sell items including watches, mugs, clothing, electronics, anything you can dream of really. Once a customer purchases an item from your store, you will then purchase your item from the wholesaler and have the wholesaler mail that item to your customer directly.

You don't have to hold any inventory in your home with dropshipping or make many items from scratch. For instance, if you have a Shopify store selling watches and your wholesaler sells you watches for $15 and sells them to customers for $40, you are making $25 of profit for every watch. You also benefit from not having to pre-buy inventory, so you minimize the risk of producing a loss. What I mean by this is the traditional way to run an online store is to have an inventory for things, right? Let's stick with the same example; let's say you wanted to run an online watch business, and you bought ten watches for this season to sell at $15 each. However, by the end of the season, you only sold five watches at $40 each. Selling this way means that you spent $150 on your inventory and only made $200; that's a $50 profit, with five watches that are now out of season. Dropshipping allows you to minimize your risk by purchasing items and selling them as the orders come in, therefore, maximizing your profit. In the same example of watches, if you only had five orders for that season and bought five watches as those orders came in, you have made a $125 profit compared to the measly $50 profit. Platforms that allow you to utilize the dropshipping method are Shopify, Amazon, and Alibaba.com.

E-Commerce: Online Garage Sales

Online garage sales are exactly how they sound. You are essentially putting up the second-hand items that you no longer need to the public to buy at a discounted price. This method is by no means a strong income generation, but it is a good secondary source of income if you combine it with a steadier side gig.

You can make use of online platforms such as Offerup, eBay, Letgo, and Craigslist. These are ideal for someone who has many items that they no longer need and knows that there are some valuable things. Items that typically sell for a lot of money include; old instruments, laptops, smartphones, tablets, brand name shoes, brand name clothes, sports equipment, headphones, televisions, kitchen appliances, collector items, furniture, and car parts. The earning potential for this type of work depends on what items you are putting up for sale and how many items you can sell. If you have the skill and experience, you could take this side gig one step further and go thrifting at pawn shops and second-hand stores to identify valuables that you can buy at a low price that you can resell for more. However, this takes more effort, and you must have good knowledge of vintage items. Many people who are good at this can make upwards of $1000/week by selling vintage clothing or antiques with a lot of history. Again, if you want to run an online store of your used items as a side gig, make sure it's not the online one as it is not as reliable as other types of income.

If you have artistic talent and have hobbies making art, running your own Etsy online store is an amazing option for you. For instance, if you have a hobby in making pottery and have gotten a lot of praise for your work, you can start your own Etsy store by selling pottery items that you have made in the past and open yourself up to commission pieces as well. Etsy is a fantastic way to make money if you are already doing your hobby regardless if it makes you money or not. You can have fun and improve your artistic ability while making some cash.

The earning potential for this is difficult to calculate as it highly depends on how successful your sales are and how you are pricing your items. For example, let's say you like to make mugs when you are doing pottery, and you make around five mugs per week. If you sold them on Etsy for $25 each and managed to sell 4 per week, you are making around $100/week and $400/month. Again, it's not a huge amount of income if your Etsy store isn't making huge sales, but it's good money considering that this is your hobby, and you were going to make these items anyway.

E-Commerce: Print On Demand (POD)

The third type of online store you can run is a print on demand (POD) business. POD is similar to dropshipping but requires your artistic and design abilities. What POD entails is selling prints that you have designed. The products could range from your paintings, drawings, graphic design, etc. You are then selling your designs printed on items of the customers' choice like posters, phone cases, t-shirts, tapestries, and many other options. You can choose only to sell one form of a product like specifically phone cases, or you can sell your designs on any imaginable printable surface. POD is ideal for someone who has a strong artistic ability to create designs. Depending on the popularity of your art, this can be a business with extremely high earning potential.

The costs simply consist of the items you want to print on (e.g., t-shirts, phone cases) and a company to do the actual printing itself. For instance, if a printing company agrees to print your design for $10 on a t-shirt and the t-shirt costs $5, the total cost for your t-shirt + design is $15. If you are selling those shirts for $40, you are bringing in $25 of profit. Again, the great part about this is similar to drop shipping; you only have to pay for the cost of the orders WHEN you get the orders. Paying upon order prevents you from holding a stock of different sized t-shirts with different prints, which will cost you a fortune if the business is slow. You only need to pay for costs when you get an actual order, which will guarantee your profit. Platforms that support this type of online store include Printful.com, Printify.com, and Teespring.com.

As a creative person, this side gig is highly beneficial for creating and selling tees or merchandise you create. This option is especially beneficial for those who may already pursue creative endeavors, such as if you are a musician, for example. That way, you can sell merchandise for your band.

If you already have an online platform that markets your work, it is good to add an online store to do POD business. You can sell your band logo and album covers in the form of t-shirts and other merchandise! Having multiple stores can increase your streams of passive income. That way, you still have plenty of time to pursue other side gigs to make you money.

E-Commerce: Clothing Sales

If you own a few sets of fancier or more expensive attire that you may only use a few times a year, this option can be great for you. If you are very interested in fashion and have a closet full of high-end clothes that you don't have the opportunity to wear a lot, this is also a great option for you.

If this is the case, you have enough resources to start your online store of renting or selling your clothes. We won't talk too much about selling your clothes in this subchapter as we talked about how you could do that through various platforms earlier; let's talk about renting your clothes.

Depending on what type of clothes you have, whether it's high-end, vintage, or rare items, you could post them on platforms such as styleend.com, tradesy.com, and threadup.com.

The earning potential in this type of business is hard to estimate because it depends on what items you are looking to rent. Again, this is a type of passive income that could generate you some cash, but I would not put all my eggs in this one basket. If you have a large closet with different clothing types that would be desirable on the market, you should consider this as your online store. This option is great as there are very few operating costs, and you could generate some good money per item you rent out.

CROWDFUNDING

Utilizing a fan base that you already have is a great way to develop a side hustle while still working on your other projects! This side gig is ideal for musicians or artists, as you don't have to step away from your music to make rent or money for groceries. This section will share some examples of platforms designed to help you turn your fan base into dollars.

Crowdfunding: Patreon

The first platform we will look at is called Patreon. This platform is a way for your fans to stay connected with you and access content that they otherwise wouldn't be able to see. They can use this platform to keep up to date on your behind the scenes, your exclusive content, or your yet-to-be-released singles that they want to be the first ones to have access to. The best part about it all is that they can also feel great knowing that they are personally helping to fund you in creating the music they love.

This platform runs on membership, which means your fans will pay a monthly fee to stay connected with you. There are different membership tiers, which all include different benefits. Your fans can choose which membership tier they want, and this informs their monthly fee. For example, your first tier of membership can include access to a community group chat as well as a free mp3 download, and your second tier can include these things as well as access to a monthly live video chat. Deciding on your tiers and what each of them includes is up to you as the musician!

Because this platform works on a monthly membership basis, your monthly revenue will be more predictable than it would with some other types of side gigs. Fans can add specific things to their monthly fees, such as merchandise or albums. You also have the option to include ads on your page or any sponsorship content that you may have, which means it has flexibility in terms of how many sources of income you want to include.

Wondering how much you can earn using Patreon? For a person who has a YouTube following of 30 thousand subscribers, you could say that about 15% of those are hardcore fans. The membership rates often range from $5 to $25, and the highest ones are somewhere around $100. As a result, if somewhere between 45 and 230 people are subscribers on Patreon, you can hope to make between $300 and $1600 monthly, depending on the number of fans that you have engaged in your monthly plans. Patreon takes about 2.5% of the membership sales to keep its platform running.

This platform allows you to connect with your fans in a closer way, as it does not use algorithms in the same way that social media platforms do. Often, on places like Instagram, your fans may miss content from you simply because of things like what they viewed last for what they view most. With Patreon, they will never miss content from you as there is no tricky algorithm that you have to work with.

Crowdfunding: Bandcamp

Bandcamp is similar in some ways to Patreon in that you can engage with your fans online, and they can support the music they love through this platform. With Bandcamp, your fans can purchase your albums or singles- and when they do, they receive a shout out on your page, showing that they supported you. You can sell your merchandise, digital downloads, vinyl albums, and tickets to your shows all in one place.

On Bandcamp, your band gets a profile on which you can display your albums, cover art, and a little blurb about you. Fans can follow you to have your updates show up on their home feed, and that way, they can stay on top of new releases. Fans can also create a Wish List to combine all of the tracks or albums they love and hope to purchase. When they purchase them, they can instantly stream tracks straight from the app or download them onto their phone or computer.

The great thing about Bandcamp is that you get to set your prices and change them at your will. You also have the option to set a minimum price and give fans the ability to pay more if they want to support your music. You can set your prices in whatever currency you like. Bandcamp makes 15% of your digital music sales and 10% of your sale for merchandise up to $100 only. There are incentives for reaching a high number of sales, as the fee lowers by 5% after an income of $5000. You get paid 48 hours after a sale, and they pay through PayPal. According to Bandcamp, their platform has helped fans pay artists about $5.3 million per month, and they have sold 30 000 records per month.

If you want to subscribe to the Pro version of the platform, there is a monthly fee of $10 per month, but you have extra features like your own unique domain and video hosting ad-free, among others.

On Bandcamp, fans don't have to search you out, as it comes with a "suggested" feature and a discovery page. The applications select the recommendations that fans see on these pages based on similar music that people have been listening to, so there is the opportunity to reach new fans and have people discover and fall in love with your music and your band for the first time.

Crowdfunding: Tipeee

Tipeee is a UK-based platform that got its name because it works through tipping. Tipeee is another platform for musicians designed after the type of tips you would give when passing a street performer on the street. If you hear a musician you like, you will drop a couple of euros into their hat after listening for a few minutes, and then you would go about your day. This platform works similarly to Bandcamp as it gives you the option to tip the creators that you see whose content you enjoy. There are many different sorts of creators on Tipeee, one of which is musicians. If you already have a fan base, you can tell them to check you out on Tipeee, and they can support you directly in this way.

On this platform, you create an artist page that includes a little bit about you and what you do, and what fans can expect from your page, such as how often you release new content or what type of content they can expect. When your fans see your Tipeee page and the content that it includes, they can tip your specific content once, repeatedly, or they can tip you monthly. You get paid all of your tips at the end of each month via PayPal. Tipeee takes 8% of your tips to keep it going. Since it is a platform based in the UK, the tips are in euros. When people tip, they can set an amount for their tip, and if people tip over a certain amount, you can offer an incentive like an exclusive song download or something of the sort.

The benefits of using Tipeee are that new people can discover your content daily, as they can browse the platform in search of new people to watch and enjoy. You can also offer exclusive songs and videos to your fans while giving them a method to support the music they love, unlike free platforms like YouTube. While Tipeee is also free, having the option to tip gives your most dedicated fans a way to thank you and give back.

All of the above methods are great ways to keep doing what you love and creating your music without sacrificing it to pay your bills. These methods are great options for people who just aren't comfortable spending more time on their side gig than their creative endeavors, as this type of side gig combines both!

LESSONS AND INSTRUCTION

In this section, we will be exploring all the side gigs that have to do with education, teaching, and tutoring. In our modern society, there is more than one way to learn a certain topic. Popular subjects like languages, especially English, are often taught by people in America, Canada, and Europe to other people from countries who want to learn English. Moreover, online tutoring is a popular income method, especially in math, science, and language studies. As long as you have some post-secondary education, you will qualify for most online teaching and tutoring jobs.

Tutoring

Tutoring can range from school subjects like math and science to teaching languages. English teaching is a growing side hustle that makes enough money for someone to live in full time. The beauty of teaching English online is that you don't even have to leave the comfort of your own home, and you can choose which hours work for you.

There are several different tutoring options, depending on whether you want to start your own tutoring business or work for someone else. There is also an option for tutoring as a source of passive income right off the bat. We will look at these different options below;

Tutoring Platforms

Let's talk a little about tutoring first, as this is the least intensive side gig in this chapter. Tutoring is an amazing side gig that could bring in a significant amount of income. You can find these opportunities through independent tutoring companies or other platforms like Wyzant and GlassGap.

Tutoring can be done in person or online, depending on your preferences. Online tutoring is more flexible as you can do it from your own home, but numerous tutoring companies in most cities hire tutors on an hourly basis to meet students' needs. Depending on your education level, you could tutor students from the levels of elementary school, high-school, and post-secondary school. The higher level the education is, the higher you will get paid on an hourly basis. You can take a look at some in-person tutoring opportunities by looking them up based on where you live. If there are many high schools or well-known universities in your area, the chances are that many businesses are looking to hire tutors for various subjects.

The above options are highly dependent on where you are located, so you can spend your own time researching which options you have. Let's talk a little about online tutoring. Online tutoring is essentially the same as in-person tutoring except for the fact that you are doing it over video conferencing rather than sitting face to face. With online tutoring, the possibility of subjects widens even more. Now you have different options to teach multiple languages, the most popular being English and other subjects that may differ from what local schools teach. Some of the most well-known tutoring platforms include tutor.com and pearson.com. Let's take a look at each platform and see what they have to offer.

- Tutor.com

*T*utor.com is a large platform that offers tutoring services to pretty much every subject imaginable. The subjects that they cover include; math (everything from algebra to calculus to statistics to middle-grade math), science (biology, chemistry, physics), English, Social studies, AP support (calculus, physics, biology), SAT/test prep, foreign languages, and business.

In terms of earning potential, online tutoring does not pay as much as in-person tutoring because you need to go through an agency. Many tutors reported making around $15 per hour using tutor.com, which is significantly less than tutoring in person. However, the flexibility is much higher, so you wouldn't need to leave the comfort of your own home, and you can build your schedule much easier.

- Pearson.com

Pearson.com is a unique way to make money in the tutoring/teaching field. Rather than teaching students on various subjects, Pearson hires many online test-scorers to mark tests and exams. Virtually anyone can do this.

The one downfall to this is that the earning potential is much lower compared to teaching and tutoring. Most Pearson test scorers make anywhere from $12 - $13 per hour. However, you do get the benefit of working from home, so you get to enjoy your flexibility. Lastly, since tests only happen at certain times of the year, there will be times where there isn't much to do, so this is not a steady side gig that can generate your income all year round. Tutoring and teaching can give you a steady flow of money throughout most of the year, but test marking and grading will only be for a few months between September – August.

- VIPKid

Platforms like VIPKid pays their online English teachers anywhere from $17 - $22 per hour. The beauty of teaching English online is that you don't even have to leave the comfort of your own home, and you can choose which hours work for you. Meanwhile, tutoring can be done online or in-person, depending on which company you work for. If you are tutoring for a high school student, the average tutor gets paid anywhere between $30 - $40 per hour. Just by doing 10 hours of it a week can bring you $300 - $400 per week of extra income; that's $900 - $1600 per month.

CREATING ONLINE COURSES

This type of side gig is a new addition to the world of side gigs and has increased in popularity over the last 1 – 2 years. These types of platforms offer courses to people who require them to qualify for jobs and further education. Platforms like udemy.com, teachable.com, and foundr.com offer courses that are made by other people at a discounted rate to either help people catch up on their credits or give them a certification that will allow them to qualify for their line of work. Depending on what education you have or if there is a demand for online music courses, these would apply to most musicians looking for side gigs, especially if they had a passion or knack for teaching.

Skillshare

Skillshare is an example of a platform that allows you to make passive income by simply creating courses for others to learn things you are passionate about. This platform is a great way to make money on the side, as you simply create a course, upload it and wait for people to purchase it. This way, you can sit back and make money once you create your course, and once it is completed and uploaded, you are finished. You can make as many or as few courses as you like, depending on how many areas of expertise you have. Skillshare is primarily focused on creative industries. For example, there are photography courses, graphic design, drawing, photoshop, animation, productivity, etc.

Thinkific

Thinkific is similar to Skillshare in that you create and upload courses, but Thinkific contains a much wider variety of course material. For example, sports and fitness, cooking, music instruction, business, marketing, and even things as specific as food photography. There is something for everyone on Thinkific, which is why this is a great option for people with niche skills or knowledge areas, especially if you have several different areas of knowledge that you can work with.

Udemy.com

Specific to Udemy.com, you can build your courses on virtually any topic possible and charge a price that you deem fair. You will get paid depending on how many people pay for your courses. Some courses are worth more than others, and people report to make anywhere between $1500 - $3000 per month for their work.

This income is highly dependent on how much you promote your courses and how many people require this type of training. In some ways, if you are only selling your course work, I would say Udemy.com is a great way to generate passive income because you won't have to do much after posting your course online for sale. However, it is not a reliable source of income as your pay will change drastically depending on how many purchases you get that month. I would keep this type of work as a source of passive income and have multiple other active income sources to generate the cash flow you need. This method definitely won't hurt to try out, especially if you already have course material at hand that you know inside and out. For instance, if you are a musician, you may know the basics of music and scales inside and out, so it will take you not much time to create a solid music foundation course.

Teachable.com

Let's talk a little about teachable.com. Teachable.com is a platform where a person can sell and create online courses for free. It allows you to build your own course website, host your content, and charge students interested in it for the course when they purchase it. Again, this is similar to Udemy as it's a great source of passive income because once you finish building your course, all you have to do is wait for it to be purchased. However, the business will heavily depend on your course's popularity and how many prospective students are in the realm of what your course offers. It is unknown so far for teachable in terms of earning potential due to the high variance from person to person. You can essentially make $0 if your course does not generate any students or interest, but some people have made over $18,000 in less than a month due to their course popularity. I'd like to drill in the point that this is a great way as a passive source of income but is highly unreliable if you want to make it your active side hustle source.

Foundr.com

Foundr.com is a resource aimed at people looking to build their own online business but need the guidance and knowledge others possess. Using the Foundr platform, you can make money by posting courses, articles, and teaching blogs about how one can jumpstart their own business. This platform isn't as popular compared to udemy and teachable due to its specialized nature. In Udemy and teachable, you can create and sell courses for virtually everything, while Foundr is focused on content related to entrepreneurship.

If you are a creative person, you may or may not have experience in this area. My recommendation would be to utilize the skills you already have through your previous education or your music skills, create courses that you're familiar with at ease, and put them up for sale as a type of passive income.

Create Your Own Business

Another option you have that is similar to the above is to create courses that you can use as a passive income source, but doing so without using a platform. That way, you won't have to pay fees to the platform to host your courses. The challenge here will be finding clients to purchase your courses, but if you are confident that you can develop leads and find business, this could be a great option for you. You can do this by hosting courses on your own website and including a payment option.

Overall, course creation side gigs are beneficial to those who have a passion for teaching and are semi-skilled in course creation. This type of work gives the freelancer a great opportunity to make large sums of money, but there is a high-risk factor. If you put in 5 hours building your course for sale and you don't make any sales at all, then you just lost out on the time you put in when you could have used that time for other side gigs with a guaranteed return. As I mentioned throughout this chapter, don't use online course creations as your main income source. Combine it with other sources and analyze how well your sales are doing in the background before putting all your eggs in one basket. Keep in mind that flexibility is great in course creation gigs. Due to its nature, you can do this type of work anytime you want as long as you have a computer that will allow you to do so. There are no tight deadlines, and you can post courses for sale whenever you want. This option could be a very good option for a fairly busy creative who wants a passive income source to pay their bills.

STARTING A COACHING BUSINESS

In this section, we will be focusing on another specific type of side hustle – coaching. To begin, I am going to explain what coaching entails. We will get more specific by learning about different coaching opportunities later on in this section. Still, we will begin by discussing the side hustle of creating your own coaching business. This kind of business will likely begin as an active source of income that you use as a side hustle, and when you grow your business to an adequate size, you can hire people to work for you while you collect the income passively.

If you are looking to start your own coaching business, you will act as the coach and find clients to help. Ideally, you must have a plethora of experience yourself in demanding feels like business or sports. Clients typically seek different coaches as they have difficulty relaying their problems, feelings, and experiences to those who don't have the experience. For instance, an Olympic swimmer may struggle to find someone to talk to about the pressure and stress they feel about the upcoming Olympics. However, a life coach who may have had experience in professional sports has the experience to provide them good insight and builds a plan that makes sense for that individual. Although you may not be an expert in professional sports, if you have been in the workforce for a while or have had a good education, then there is likely a niche of coaching that you would be suitable for. For instance, some people who found success working in a sales job may be interested in starting a business coaching business. In comparison, someone who has found success as a Yoga teacher or enthusiast may be interested in starting a spiritual coaching business.

There are many different types of coaching businesses, and there is something for everyone; it is just a matter of finding out what makes the most sense for your knowledge and skills.

If you are thinking about starting your own coaching business in the first place, you probably want to know how coaching compares to a career during these unstable times of the economy. The best part about this is that coaching is gaining an excellent reputation as a profession, probably because of the uncertainties in our economy, forced career changes, and businesses' drastic efforts to make their operations more efficient and productive during numerous financial challenges. In terms of statistics, the coaching industry in 2012 brought i2 billion spread amongst approximately 50,000 coaches.

You may already know that coaches set their rates and their rates tend to differ a lot. Some coaches may charge $25 per hour, while some may charge $300+ per hour. After coming out from a certification program, the standard hourly rates for certain coaches can be anywhere from $100 per hour to $150 per hour.

The most significant differentiating factor between coaching rates depends on the type of coaching that you are doing. Although there are numerous different coaching types, the industry includes life coaching, business coaching, and executive coaching.

A recent study on the coaching industry found that the average income for coaches who worked full time was over $80,000. For coaches who did it part-time, it brought in revenue of around $25,000 per year. For you to have a good understanding of what type of coaching brings in the most income, let's take a look at some of the top coaches in our industry today that are making over $100,000.

Below I have outlined what the relationship between the coach and client aims to be:

- The ability of the coach to create, identify and clarify the client's visions

- The ability of the coach to use their expertise to change any goals that they feel fit
- The ability of the coach to encourage the client's growth and self-discovery
- The ability of the coach to nurture strategies and an action plan that is most suitable for the goals, vision, and personality of the client
- The coach holds the client account to increase their productivity

Those are just the most common reasons why people hire coaches to work with them towards their goals. The main goal of a life coach is to help the client maximize their potential. According to research and statistics, hiring a coach is the most effective way to increase productivity. Statistics show that productivity increases by a whopping 88% when a person hires a life coach to assist them, compared to only 22%, without a coach and using hands-on training alone.

This section will teach you about the different opportunities that exist if you wish to choose coaching as your side hustle. We have already looked at life coaching, and we will examine a few more now. There are many different types of coaching side hustles to choose from, and this section will help you narrow down your choices based on your experience levels.

Life Coaching

Life coaches are the most common type of coaches when it comes to side hustles. A life coach is a person who helps people identify their goals and builds a plan for them to take action towards achieving those goals. However, this may sound like a foreign concept to many people, people who have demanding jobs need the experience, support, perspective, and insight of a life coach. People like professional athletes benefit significantly from hiring a life coach. The same is true for executives, CEOs, or entrepreneurs that run large and successful companies. The definition of a life coach differs based on what the person's specific goals are. A life coach's job is to counsel people dealing with a range of professional and personal issues. Life coaching includes giving clients advice, counseling, mentoring, and administering a bit of therapy.

Most people would hire a life coach to help them with specific projects, transitions, or personal goals. The coach's responsibility is to help you grow by assessing your current situation, limiting beliefs, and other challenges. The coach will then create a customized plan that they design to help you achieve your goals.

Corporate/ Career Coaching

Career coaches are focused on helping people that are seeking career advice. These coaches use a very solution-oriented approach to help clients define, redefine, and achieve their goals related to their current working situation's professional objectives. For example, a career coach can help people figure out what type of job they're looking for next to grow their careers. They specialize in giving people advice based on what their current working situation is. They could be executives, employees, or freelancers. Regardless, career coaches help these people develop skills like leadership, stress management, self-confidence, interpersonal skills, and conflict-management skills.

Depending on the clients' needs, the career coach's responsibilities, tasks, and services will differ. However, the core coaching process is still the same in all cases. Here are some of the primary responsibilities of a career coach:

- Running meetings with clients to understand what their professional goals are professional background, and education level.
- The career coach is skilled in recognizing what the client's needs, difficulties, opportunities, and skills are
- The career coach utilizes specialized tools like assessments and vocational tests to figure out what their client's skill levels are
- The career coach helps the client find and discover career opportunities by doing market research
- Providing the client with recommendations and tips on how to keep a job and move up within a company
- If their client is an employer, the career coach will advise them on common employment-related issues and best HR practices, this includes:
- Improving profitability and efficiency, increasing overall satisfaction, and improving the work environment
- Tracking the performance of company/employees, creating reports, and helping the client establish measurable goals
- Assisting clients with the job hunting process
- Reviewing resume and applications by suggesting improvements to improve their chances
- Helping clients with interview preparation by giving tips, advice, and practice through the use of mock interviews
- Educating the client on the best practices of networking within their field

- Identifying what their client's needs are and assisting them in other areas like their finance and their overall health
- Running educational presentations through the use of workshops and webinars

Financial Coaching

A financial coach is responsible for helping their clients with money management basics. They work with clients struggling with their money management or simply just have an unhealthy relationship with money. A financial coach's primary responsibility is to help their clients develop better and healthier money managing habits that are sustainable. Financial coaches spend a lot of time educating their clients on personal finance basics and work hand in hand with them to create a financial plan to help them achieve their personal goals. They also focus heavily on empowering their clients to be responsible for their spending actions and help them develop accountability for themselves.

On average, financial coaches work with each of their clients over several weeks. They would meet with their clients every week to advise them on their finances and check in on their progress. The process that financial coaches use typically consists of three steps. The first step is to help them become more aware of their spending habits by tracking their spending to see for themselves. The second step is to help the client build their own financial goals, whether it's to pay off debt, save up for a property, or simply create a budget. The last step in this process is for the financial coach to help their clients build out sustainable plans and hold them accountable to follow those plans.

You might be wondering what the difference is between a financial coach and a financial advisor at this point. The main difference is that a financial coach helps teach those who aren't strong in money and finance management to better manage their money, while financial advisors advise you to grow and invest your money. Typically, financial coaches work with clients who don't have many assets and need to generate more financial stability for themselves. While financial advisors usually make their money by charging a percentage of the money your assets are generating, financial coaches usually charge by the hour or have a flat retainer fee.

Financial coaching has the flexibility of being done in person, over the phone, or via video conferencing. The kind of meetings you hold is quite flexible as there isn't a need for the financial coach to see the client face to face. Since these sessions' purpose is to focus on money management, there isn't a need to be face-to-face.

If you think financial coaching is your niche, you may be interested in specializing in it even further. You could specialize your financial coaching services towards people looking to get out of debt or looking to save up for a down payment, or those who simply are bad with money. You can identify which further specializations are the most suitable for you by assessing your own experience. Have you ever experienced getting yourself out of debt? Have you ever saved up for your down payment? Or are you someone who used to be terrible with their money but now have multiple assets?

These are all things you could consider before choosing what your coaching type will be.

Performance Coaching

Performance coaches are focused on helping clients that need to improve their performance or abilities for a specific task that they likely have or want a career in. For instance, performance coaches can help a client who is a professional snowboarder and is looking to discover their full potential to reach their goals. Their goals can range from simply winning a competition or qualifying for the winter Olympics.

Consequently, performance coaching also helps people that aren't athletes. For instance, writers can seek a performance coach's help to get an idea of their full potential when writing. The performance coach can help assess where they are in terms of their writing skill, assess their work, and help guide the client into creating a vision and a set of goals that can be accompanied by an action plan. Performance coaching is one of those coaching types where it's almost necessary to specialize even further. Some performance coaches only coach people in the performing arts like ballet, while other performance coaches may focus on half-pipe snowboarding.

Performance coaches are responsible for facilitating conversations with their clients so that the clients are encouraged to set goals that are achievable and are working towards a larger goal. These coaches also help their clients build their self-awareness to identify and overcome any challenges and obstacles they may face when looking to improve their desired skills.

Performance coaching is mainly non-directive, which means that the coach does not tell the client exactly what to do or do something. However, performance coaching focuses on helping the client if they have lost their way or need advice on some issues. This type of coaching is better conducted via in-person sessions because they need to assess the client's skill level at a certain activity. It is also crucial that the coach helps the client discover things that they didn't even know that they needed to know. For this, the coach and the client need to have meetings face to face as body language speaks loudly for uncovering growth areas.

If you are looking to do performance coaching, it is ideal for specializing even further within a skill that you are confident that you have a lot of knowledge. For instance, if you have been a snowboarder your whole life and want your side hustle to be performance coaching, it will be beneficial for you to advertise your coaching business as performance coaching specializing in snowboarding. Due to your history and experience with this sport, you can gain many credibilities when marketing your services and pitching your ideas to clients.

Performance coaching can be done individually, in groups, or in corporate situations. It is mostly done individually, but corporate companies may seek out this type of service. For instance, dance studios or boot camp companies may seek out a performance coach to help their clients further build upon their skills.

Spiritual Coaching

A spiritual coach focuses on helping the client connect with their inner-self. These coaches help their clients change, navigate, and re-direct their lives to discover their desires, goals, dreams, and break out of any limiting beliefs. Unlike the other types of coaching we've discussed, spiritual coaching's main goal is to help people get in touch with themselves. A person may want to get in touch with themselves because they have lost their way in life and need to re-discover who they are, or it could be someone that's gone through an impactful experience and want to explore new beginnings.

Spiritual coaches use a more holistic approach with their clients. They tend to help their clients discover their operating system that is under their consciousness. Spiritual coaches help people discover more than just who they are on the surface. Here are the areas that a spiritual coach can help their clients with:

- Spiritual coaches help their clients to live consciously.
- Spiritual coaches help clients build a connection to their inner-self.
- Spiritual coaches help clients find out their true selves and help them connect to their purpose in life.
- Spiritual coaches help clients heal old wounds, release trauma, clear stagnation, and open energy blocks.
- Spiritual coaches help clients have a deeper connection with themselves.

Don't mix up spiritual coaching with life coaching. Life coaches work to help clients change their lives for the better, primarily concerning their home life, relationships, families, and health. A spiritual coach explores further than just the physical parts of people's lives and dives into the 'why' behind everything they do. Spiritual coaching helps the client discover their depth and helps guide the client as they journey through self-discovery. All these changes run deeper than just surface level, but they all involve finding the underlying understanding of a person's being that contributes to long-lasting happiness.

Spiritual coaching can happen in person, over the phone, and via video conferencing. It can also be in the form of individual sessions, group sessions, and corporate sessions. Since spiritual coaches focus on everything below the surface, there isn't a need for sessions to happen in person, so normally sessions over the phone will suffice. If you think that spiritual coaching is your niche, you know what I'm about to say next – you can specialize even further. You can specialize in your spiritual coaching services to help people move on from trauma or help people break away from the norm and discover who their inner-self is. Remember, the best way to identify your second specialization is to look back onto your own experience and assess what areas you feel confident in coaching others.

Wellness Coaching

Wellness coaches help their clients by helping them build sustainable and healthy behavior in their day to day lives. They do this by helping the clients identify their skills, strengths, and resources and help them create a vision of who they want to be and guide them towards it. A wellness coach usually applies the principles and methods that include cognitive-behavioral approaches, structured journaling, positive psychology, and solution-based approaches. These are all techniques that help the client realize what they need to do to achieve their goals. It is not by any means the coach telling them how to change their lives, but more so the coach guides them into realizing what changes they need to make for themselves.

Like I mentioned numerous times, there isn't a prerequisite to becoming a coach. There is no prerequisite for becoming a wellness coach; anyone can do it as long as they are in a position where they can influence and help others through science-based tools.

For instance, many organizations, especially health and fitness organizations, hire a full-time wellness coach. In other cases, some people may already be working in a health organization and have the skills to be a life coach, thus choosing to cross-train within their organization to add wellness coaching to their skill set. Adding this will help them to grow their responsibilities at work or to start their side hustle. These people who usually get cross-trained as a wellness coach include; therapists, medical assistants, nurses, massage therapists, personal trainers, and fitness teachers (yoga, spin class, Pilates, etc.).

Wellness coaches help clients make changes to their present wellness. The clients can range from people who have a smoking or drinking habit to someone who is perfectly physically healthy but wants to improve their mental wellness. Wellness coaches can take on clients that are individuals, groups, and corporate. They have the opportunity to work with individual clients who may be looking to improve their health, for instance, a lifetime smoker who is looking to change their habits. Consequently, they can also work for a corporate company like a Sales company in a very high-stress environment and is looking to hire a wellness coach to help teach their employees to cope with stress and pressure daily. Most wellness coaches like to do their sessions face to face, as it is important to them to physically see their client's health and wellness in a person. However, video conferencing will suffice if their clients live far away, but telephone sessions are rare with wellness coaches.

PASSIVE INCOME IDEAS- IN PERSON

THIS CHAPTER WILL DISCUSS some of the most popular side gigs and passive income sources on the market right now that do not use the internet but instead use tangible resources like your car or property. Examples include renting out your car for others to use, using rideshare platforms like Uber and Lyft, or using your car to perform delivery services. The second most popular side gig uses a property you own to make money, which we will discuss later in this chapter. Finally, we will end this chapter by looking at arbitrage (the purchasing and selling commodities to make money) and how this can be a lucrative side hustle for you! Let's begin the chapter!

USING YOUR CAR

This type of work is one of the most reliable sources of income in the world of side gigs due to its huge client demand and popularity in major metropolitan cities. You can build your schedule, which adds a ton of flexibility, and the income is very steady during prime hours like before or after work or on the weekends.

The earning potential is also quite high in this type of side gig; drivers report making anywhere from \$11 per hour to \$29 per hour. Factoring in its high level of flexibility and easiness of the job, that's great money! Let's begin to look at the various ways you could make money using your car.

Car Rental

The first way you can make a side gig out of your car is to rent your actual vehicle. It's just what you're thinking; you are essentially acting as a car rental company but only with your vehicle.

Using a car is a great passive source of income as you don't need to do anything besides confirming your customers, and you receive money from them using your car.

Unlike ridesharing gigs like Uber and Lyft, you don't need to put in the hours to generate income actively; as long as your car is in decent shape, you can make money just by letting someone else use it temporarily. This method is a great option for making good money by renting your car out if you don't use it a lot.

Platforms such as Getaround, Turo, and Hyrecar pay you money to rent out your car just like any car rental company would, and you essentially get paid for doing nothing at all!

Average car renters make anywhere between $500 - $800 per month renting out their car. If you rent it out 100% of the month, you will make more money than only renting it 50% of the time. The car model makes a difference, so if you have a fancy car like a Tesla, you can make a premium.

- Turo

At the moment, it seems like Turo is the most popular platform in terms of car rentals, so that is one platform you can look into if you are interested in renting out your car. This platform also comes with a nice feature to estimate how much your specific make and car model can make for you. This feature is ideal if you want to estimate its income before diving right into this type of side gig. With its increase in popularity throughout major cities, especially those with high tourism, you can make some serious cash by just letting someone drive your car for a few days! Not only does this help you make some extra cash if you are currently financing or leasing your car, but you can also use this money to help break-even with your purchase. Two birds, one stone!

- Getaround

Getaround is a similar platform to Turo in that it offers the same services. It does not have the same feature as Turo with the estimation calculator. Still, you could consider cross-posting your car into multiple car-share websites to maximize the number of times your car can be rented by maximizing your reach. The earning potential is highly dependent on what type of car you have and the demand in your city, but most car-renters report making anywhere from $500 - $800 per month.

- HyreCar

HyreCar is an interesting platform as it is a combination of Turo and Getaround mixed with Uber and Lyft. Its services are specialized towards people who don't have a car but want to pursue rideshare jobs. HyreCar allows people to rent Uber/Lyft qualified cars to use Uber and Lyft to make money. This platform is an option for you as well in terms of side gigs.

If you don't have a car, you can rent a car starting from $25 per day and generate income through rideshare or food delivery services. If you DO have a car of your own, you can make money by posting on HyreCar and renting it to someone else who wants to use it for Uber or Lyft to generate their income.

Again, if renting out your car is an option you are looking to pursue, cross-posting on these sites will help you generate the most business. Remember that renting out your car is a passive income. It allows you to do something else to make more money as a more primary and active source of money.

Starting your Own Rental Business

The final option for renting your car is to create your own car rental business. If you have multiple cars that you don't mind renting out, you can create your own business. By doing it this way, you don't have to pay fees to the platform such as Turo or

Getaround, but it will come with its own set of challenges. The great thing about using a platform like Turo is that the insurance for your renter is included. If you are planning on creating your own business, there will be many more logistical issues for you to look into, such as insurance, car storage, and so on. If you have ample resources at your fingertips, this could be a great option for you, but ensure that you look into everything involved before pursuing this option.

Rideshare

Ridesharing is probably the most popular form of side gig available on the market right now. Working as a rideshare driver is a common and great way to make extra money as you can build your schedule, and drivers average anywhere from $11 per hour to $29 per hour depending on what time of day they decide to operate.

Companies like Uber and Lyft are great platforms to get started with if you already own a vehicle and have a valid driver's license. Not only is this method a great way for you to make an extra few hundred dollars a month, but you are also helping out people who need a ride. This side gig has gotten so popular and has brought in so much income that some people treat this side-gig as their main job.

If you are a person who is busy with your work during the daytime, you can add a second source of income by providing rideshare services on evenings and weekends. If you put an extra 10 hours a week on your evenings and weekends to do this, you can make anywhere from $110 - $290 per week. That is an extra monthly income of $440 - $1160. Depending on where you live, you pay less tax working as a contractor to bring in more money to tax and net income ratio.

If you were to start a rideshare side business using existing platforms like Uber and Lyft, you are already guaranteed clients as that's the platform's job- to match you with people who need a ride. This method is a quicker way to gain side business income while still working your full-time job. As I said, Rideshare drivers can make anywhere between $110 - $290 per week working part-time, which is an extra monthly income of $440 - $1160.

Keep in mind that this is an active source of income, but it is a great way to start a side gig and make extra money that will allow you to transition to a passive income source like the car rental income, as discussed above.

- Uber

Uber is the original player in the rideshare game and shares a very similar platform to Lyft. As long as you have a decently modern and clean car, you qualify to drive for Uber. You can build your schedule simply by turning on your Uber application when you are ready to drive and turning it off when you are finished.

There are also other ways to make more money, such as making your car complete with refreshments to generate more trips. Another way to maximize your income is by driving during surge times where prices are higher. The flexibility in this type of work is very high, as you can work whenever you want. The only downside to this is that you have to be there physically, so you don't get the luxury of staying at home to work like other remote jobs.

- Lyft

The rideshare platform *Lyft* is *Uber's* biggest competitor and, in terms of business model and platform, is virtually the same. They do pay at slightly different rates, but the difference is very small, and most people don't notice.

Many drivers will drive for both Uber and Lyft to maximize the amount of business they get. The qualifications are the same for Lyft, where you need to have a decently modern car that is clean and in good condition to qualify. Other than that, you can clock in and clock out whenever you like. Both Lyft and Uber drivers make a percentage of what the platform charges the passenger. The faster and more rides you can get done, the more money per hour you are making.

By any means, make sure you are still driving safely, but you could maximize your income by driving passengers promptly. Keep in mind that ratings also matter. Based on your service and driving ability, passengers can give you a score from one star (poor) to five stars (excellent). This rating affects the number of passengers you get matched with and could make or break the business flow for you.

Delivery Services

Another very popular side gig these days that you can do with a car or some means of transportation is acting as a delivery service. People may need many different kinds of delivery services, but the most popular in today's world is food delivery.

Services like UberEats, Foodora, and Doordash frequently employ a team of food delivery people to pick up food from restaurants and deliver it to the person who ordered it. This type of side hustle originally started with delivering food from established restaurants but now have evolved into delivering everyday items like groceries, over the counter medicine, and alcohol.

If you own a vehicle or a bicycle and enjoy roaming through the city you live in, you can sign up and make some money doing so. The type of transportation you use will largely depend on your resources, but there is no shame in starting on a bicycle until you have enough money to buy a car. These couriers have reported that they make around $12 - $20 an hour. If you dedicate an extra 10 hours of your week to this side hustle, you can make an extra $120 - $200 per week, grossing $480 - $800 of extra monthly income. This method is not a passive source of income in any way, but it is a second active income that you can add to your earnings on your way to developing passive income.

- Creating Your Own Delivery Business

If you have the means, you can create your own delivery business, which will allow you to make passive income. This delivery business could be a courier service, a food delivery service, or any other delivery service type. If you create a business like this, you can employ drivers and delivery persons, which will allow you to take a more hands-off approach and make passive income.

RENTING SPACE THAT YOU OWN MONTHLY

A great way to earn passive income is by collecting rent every month on a property you own. You can list a room, a house, or an apartment on any rental site, like craigslist, and find a tenant to rent your place monthly for a yearly contract. This method is a great, hassle-free, and hands-off way to make passive income. Before we delve into some of the other ways to make money using a property you own, I have a few notes to make on buying property.

A NOTE ON BUYING PROPERTY

As I mentioned, investing in a property is a great and secure way to grow your money in the long-term. If you are in a position to buy a property, I strongly suggest it. Even if you are not ready to live in a property that you own, there are numerous ways to turn this into a passive income source for yourself. One way to turn this into passive income is by using it as a rental property. Doing this can bring you rental income or cover your mortgage payments for you. The second way is by simply investing your money and waiting for your house's value to grow. When this happens, you can sell, and you will make a lump-sum of money that you earned passively.

It can be challenging to make enough money to invest in a property, but any of the side gigs in this book can help you to earn and save passive income that will bring you closer to buying a property. For example, if you had enough money for a down payment for a property, think $50,000 - $100,000 at least, then you could invest in a home and turn it into a property where it generates rental income for you. Let's say you got a decent mortgage from your local bank, and you put down a $50,000 down payment for a $300,000 home. Now let's say you agreed to a monthly payment of $2,500 to your bank plus a 2.5% interest rate for ten years, which leads you to pay around $2560 a month. Since property prices tend to increase with time depending on where you live naturally, it's safe to say that your $300,000 investment could become a $400,000 investment in a few years. If you rent out your new property to tenants that cover the full mortgage ($2560), this means that you are no longer making payments to the bank, the tenants are, and you get to keep your money growing on your property. By spending $50,000 on your down payment, you are generating over $300,000 of income over the next few years with a high likelihood of it becoming a property that is worth way more than $300k in a few years. Let's say in 5 years, your property value has increased to $450,000. By doing nothing at all, you have paid off $125,000 ($2500 per month x 5 years), and the value of your house has grown by $150,000. Therefore, in just five years, with minimal work, you have made $275,000. For some people, that is a decent salary of $55,000 a year for five years. All of this was made by simply having enough resources to build a strong passive income stream.

PROPERTY RENTALS

A great option for a side gig is running a property rental. This method is a great option for you if you have an extra property or an extra room in your house/apartment. Rooms and units could be rented from $50 per night to $250 per night, which brings you a weekly income of $150 - $750 if you rent a space in your own home from Friday – Monday. Various property rentals can earn you passive income, which we will look at below.

Property Rentals: Event Space

Another side gig that is a great source of passive income is to rent out event space. This way, you collect a fee for people who want to use your space to host events such as parties, weddings, or anything else. This passive income source can make you a lot of money with very minimal work required on your part.

Property Rentals: Vacation Rentals

Vacation rentals are a growing form of side-hustle, especially for people who live in high-rent cities like New York City, San Francisco, or Toronto. You can make vacation rentals a larger source of your income if you have a spare room in your home or a property that you can fix up to be rented.

Renting out your room/unit on a nightly basis can make you anywhere from $50 - $250 per night. Some people decide to rent a room in their apartment from Friday – Sunday, as most people use the weekend to have a getaway. This method allows you to maintain your vacation rental property away from your day job while making anywhere from $150/weekend to $600/weekend. You also have the flexibility of setting your nightly price, so dates with higher demand like Christmas or Spring break can be listed at a higher nightly price.

- Airbnb

Instead of paying rent or mortgage to your home while you are away, you can list it as an Airbnb or HomeAway rental for tourists or travelers to rent. Due to the increasing cost of nearly everything, people nowadays prefer to book an Airbnb compared to a hotel to save money by having the amenities to cook their food and fit more people into one space.

Property Rentals: House Sitting

House sitting is a great side-gig as you could rent out your property while you live somewhere else, and you get paid for watching over someone's home while they are away. There are many platforms such as House Sitters America and Trusted Hour Sitters that can help match people who require house sitters to people who are interested in doing it.

Often, house sitting entails watering plants, bringing in mail, and keeping the person's home safe and clean throughout their trip. Although this type of side-hustle is not as popular as the previous ones, it requires minimal effort. Further, you can incorporate other side-hustles (like renting out your own home while living at someone else's house) to maximize your income.

This method is a great way to earn passive income or to break even while you travel. This method is also great for people who don't own a property and rent an apartment. Instead of paying rent on an apartment, you can save that cost by house-sitting for someone in your city. If you don't mind moving around often, this is a great option and can help you save a significant amount of money.

ARBITRAGE

Now, let's start learning about the basics of investing. Investing is another good way to grow your money and turn it into passive income. However, certain investments can be risky so learning about the different types is important for you to decide which ones you want to pursue and which ones may require more knowledge and research. Let's take a look. Below, we will look at several forms of arbitrage investing that can lead to great passive income gains for you.

Stocks

Stocks are one of the most basic investment forms and likely the most common one you hear about. In the most basic explanation, stocks are securities that represent an ownership share in a company. Companies will issue stocks to raise money from the general public to grow and invest in their own business. Stocks are then exchanged in the stock market. The stock market, such as the New York Stock Exchange, is made up of exchanges. Stocks are listed on a specific exchange and allow sellers and buyers to come together to sell/buy shares of certain stocks. The exchange tracks the supply and demand, which usually directly relates to the price or each stock.

Stock prices fluctuate daily, and people who own stocks hope that stocks that they own will increase in value with time. For instance, if you bought a stock for company A for $20 apiece, and that stock grows to be worth $50 apiece in three years, you have made $30 over three years ($10 per year). However, stocks carry some of the highest risks than other investments, but they can also reap higher rewards. Some people look at stocks as a type of 'gambling' as it is difficult to predict the increase/decrease of stocks. Take a look at bitcoin; for example, what used to be a $7 stock grew to be worth $7000 per stock in the past few years. Although this may sound promising, it can happen the other way around too. You can buy a bitcoin stock for $7000 now and hope that it will grow to $14,000 or more. However, it could drop down back to $7, causing you to lose significant amounts of money.

Commodities

Commodities are an important part of an average American's daily life. In its simplest form, a commodity is a basic good used in commerce to interchange with other goods in the same category. For example, grains, beef, gold, natural gas, and oil are traditional commodities. For investors, commodities are an important way to diversify portfolios beyond just traditional securities. Since prices of commodities usually move in opposition to stocks, investors rely on commodities during a period of market volatility. Professional traders usually do commodity trading as it is more complicated and does require quite a bit of knowledge and education to pull off effectively. For that reason, I won't go into detail about how commodities are traded and the functions.

REIT (Real Estate Investment Trust)

REIT stands for Real Estate Investment Trust. A REIT is a company that operates, owns, or finances income-generating real estate.

*R*EITs are modeled after mutual funds and pool capital of numerous investors, allowing investors to earn dividends from various real estate investments without needing to buy, finance, or manage any of these properties themselves. Typical properties in a REIT portfolio include hotels, apartment complexes, healthcare facilities, data centers, or it can also be in the form of telecommunications such as; fiber cables and cell towers.

*R*EITs also require a bit more real-estate knowledge as some REIT portfolios are a mixed bag of different properties. I don't recommend REITs for beginner investors as there are many risk factors and areas that you must learn about them. However, many professional investors and traders swear by REITs, so if this is something you'd like to do, please do some heavy research and learn about the REITs in your market before investing any money.

Bonds

Unlike a stock, a bond is a loan taken out by a company, but instead of asking a bank for this money, they ask investors for money by asking them to purchase bonds. In exchange for capital, the company will pay an annual interest rate on the bond, annually or semi-annually, and then returns the principal loan on the maturity date. There are six features that you should look out for before purchasing a bond:

- **Maturity:** Maturity is the date when the bond is paid, and when the initial chunk of money is returned to you. Maturity is often divided up into; short-term (1 – 3 years), medium-term (10+ years), and long-term (20+ years)
- **Secured/Unsecured:** A bond can either be secured or unsecured. A secured bond promises the bondholders specific assets if the company cannot repay its obligation. This event can also be called collateral. If the bond issuer defaults, then the asset is transferred back to the investor. Unsecured bonds are the opposite. Any collateral does not back them up. These bonds will return only a little bit of your investment if the company fails.
- **Liquidation Preference:** When a company declares bankruptcy, it will repay its investors in a particular order as they liquidate their assets. Senior debt is debt that will be paid first, and junior debt will be paid last. Stockholders will then get whatever is left.
- **Coupon:** The coupon amount refers to the interest paid to bondholders either annually or semiannually. The Coupon can be referred to as the nominal yield or the 'coupon rate.' To calculate this, divide your annual payments by the face value of your bond.
- **Tax Status:** Most corporate bonds are taxable investments, but government/municipal bonds are exempt from tax. Any income or capital gains will be taxed. However, tax-exempt bonds will have a lower interest rate than taxable bonds.
- **Callability:** The company can pay off some bonds before its maturity. A company may choose to call its bonds if the interest rate allows them to borrow at better rates.

HIGH-INTEREST SAVINGS ACCOUNT

If you have a small fortune saved up, think like $20,000. You can easily put that $20,000 in high-interest savings account at your local bank and generate 2-3% interest on it monthly. Using this method, you are making $4,800 - $7,200 yearly by doing nothing at all.

If you do not have a small fortune saved up yet, any of the passive income or side hustle ideas in this book will allow you to save extra money. They will bring you closer to making passive income in the form of investment, high-interest savings account, or arbitrage- as discussed above.

PASSIVE INCOME IDEAS- SKILL REQUIRING

THIS CHAPTER WILL FOCUS on passive income sources that will allow you to use skills that you may already have. Depending on which skills you have, they can prove extremely beneficial for freelance work. We are going to look at several ways that you can use the skills to make passive income. Let's go through each of these forms of skill-based passive income and find out which ones would work best for you.

CONSULTING

Consulting can be a great side gig for those who are looking to have flexible hours and earn good money while still having time to work a full-time job. Consulting is a great option for those who have expertise in any specific area, as you can make money imparting this advice to others.

Consulting will most often begin as an active source of income. Still, after some time, you may be able to switch into a passive role, especially if you create a strong name for yourself and can start your own business or hire others to consult under your company for you.

Below, we will look at some platforms that offer consulting clients to experts in various fields. These platforms can help you get started in the world of consulting.

- Clarity.fm

Clarity is an online consulting platform that connects experts with people looking to get advice on business-related topics such as Marketing, Social Media, and Entrepreneurship, among others. If you have knowledge and experience relating to these areas, you may be able to begin making money by sharing this advice with other people! Since you are reading this book, you are likely somewhat of an entrepreneur, so you may have the skills to become an expert with Clarity. The great thing about Clarity is that it has the flexibility to allow you to be an expert in a wide variety of topics within the larger umbrellas of Sales & Marketing, Technology, Skills & Management, and Product & Design. Within these umbrellas are a wide range of topics, and many people can find topics within these that they are knowledgeable in and confident giving advice in.

To begin earning money, you sign up as An Expert, and once you go through the onboarding process, you can begin having calls with people seeking your advice. You will get paid by the minute, so you are cashing in for each minute you spend on a call with a person seeking your advice. Most people charge between $2 and $7 per minute, depending on their experience, while the occasional expert will charge $50 to $80 per minute. Your income all depends on what type of experience and education you bring to the table. Experts set their own rates, and choosing what rate to set will depend on your ability to show value. By starting somewhere around $1.60 per minute, your 30-minute call will get you $50 or so. Based on this, you can decide what to charge. Clarity pays their experts every 15 days through PayPal, and 15% of your pay is given to the company.

The majority of people who use Clarity for advice purposes are new entrepreneurs or business owners looking to filter out all of the free advice they can find online and quickly get real expert advice. By doing a quick search on the platform, you can find experts ready to advise on a vast range of topics, including the music industry, business and finance, fitness, and so on.

- Inzite.com

Inzite is another consulting platform that provides its users with advice on various topics through consultants who are experts in their field. On Inzite, the consultants are called Advisors, and the advice-seekers are called Users. Inzite includes a wide variety of experts, including coaches, mentors, and consultants that, when combined, can offer support in any area of expertise. Like Clarity, Inzite offers advice on a wide range of topics, music being one of them as there is an entire section of their Discover page titled "Arts, Music & Culture." If you are an experienced musician with advice to give, this could be a great solution for your side gig.

As an Advisor on Inzite, you can set your availability to let people know when you are available for meetings. The meetings come in the form of phone calls, instant messaging, and video chats. You have the option to offer free initial information sessions or to begin with paid sessions. To become an Advisor, you simply complete an online application form through their website, and you hear back once the application has been processed.

Most calls work on a fixed-price basis, as the duration of the call will be pre-determined. You can decide on your fixed prices for pre-determined call lengths (30min, 45 min, etc.), or you can set an hourly rate that the user would pay by the minute. If the call goes overtime, the user is charged your per-minute rate. Inzite does not have subscription fees for its Advisors' users, but it takes 15% of your earnings. The calls are free of charge as they happen on a conference line set up by the platform. Your funds are deposited into your account on the platform, after which you can withdraw them into your bank account free of charge.

- COMATCH.com

COMATCH is a consulting platform that focuses on consulting for large companies in need of business consulting. The topics of consulting that COMATCH concerns itself with are Startup Business Solutions, Management, Information Technology, Market Research, Operations and Strategy, and Finance. To work with COMATCH, you must have some business knowledge, but you may have some of this experience if you are a musical entrepreneur.

COMATCH works with large companies that submit a business proposal outlining their project and what type of consulting they require. From here, consultants are selected based on their knowledge of and experience with the project specified. The company can then choose between the submitted consultants by interviewing them over the phone or simply deciding on the best match. A contract is signed, and the consultant can begin working on the project. The platform itself is in charge of invoicing and recording all logistics to ensure that you are paid what you are owed. Your income possibilities will vary depending on your experience and the number of projects you are selected for based on how closely your skills match the current projects. It is difficult to estimate compensation as the company must first put you through their hiring process.

COMATCH began as a company in Germany but has quickly spread worldwide, including the United States. If you have skills and experience in business and would like to put these skills to use as a freelance, remote consultant, you can do so through COMATCH. Their hiring process is a little more stringent than the others, but it comes at a good price when it is time for payday. This company employs its consultants on a full-time basis. COMATCH allows musicians or any other artists to pursue their art while still making enough money to live well.

CREATING YOUR OWN CONSULTING BUSINESS

As I mentioned, consulting is a great area that can make you large sums of money. The best way to make passive income in consulting is to create your own business and hire consultants to work for you. Starting a consulting business will not be easy, but it will be well worth it in the end once you are collecting a large amount of income passively. It may be best to begin on a platform like the ones I mentioned above to get an idea of what a consulting business entails before creating your own consulting business.

- Business Consulting

One great example of a consulting business that is in high demand these days is business consulting. A business consultant focuses on helping business owners by assisting and guiding them to run their business. You will do this by clarifying their vision and aligning their business with their personal goals.

Alternatively, business consultants can help people looking to start their own business (entrepreneurs) and help guide them to follow the best business practices and help them create a vision for what they want their business to be. In simpler words, business coaches follow a process to help grow a business from its present state to where the client wants their business to be.

An essential part of business coaching is for the coach to help the client understand that any company vision and story is entirely theirs to create. Business coaches don't help their clients by creating their business stories and visions; instead, they help them discover their vision and plan for them to execute. A business coach's main role is to introduce concepts, tools, and processes to their clients that help them grow their organization and team to create a good business story and vision. Here are a few other responsibilities of a business coach:

- Optimize the alignment of the entire organization
- Increase accountability within teams and individuals in the organization
- Strengthen the company culture
- Increase the focus of the organization
- Make better decisions regarding the 'people.'
- Develop strategies that are more effective in growing the business

A business coach can target individual clients, group clients, or corporate clients. In most cases, business coaches aim to market their services to corporate clients, as that is where they can bill the most hours at the highest rates. However, there are still a plethora of clients that fall into the individual category. Most of the time, these are people who have already started their small to medium-sized businesses and are looking to grow it further by creating a vision, or the clients are people that do not have their own business yet, but their goal is to build their own. In both these cases, the business coach helps assess the client's current state in terms of their business and help them create the vision and plan needed to grow their business to a state where they want it to be.

Depending on what type of client the business coach has, they could deliver their sessions in person, over the phone, or by video conferencing. Most corporate companies that hire business coaches would require them to come into their workplace to deliver these sessions. In contrast, entrepreneur type clients may deem over the phone sessions sufficient. Business coaches typically have some sort of background or career within that field. This experience can range from having run their own business before, having worked in management or executive-level positions in the business field, or having a good grasp of how businesses work and how to grow them in size, revenue, and vision.

Like I mentioned earlier, there isn't a specific prerequisite for any type of coaching. You must assess yourself and see where your strongest skills lie to determine what coaching niche makes the most sense for you. Some business coaches specialize in coaching entrepreneurs only, while others will take established business professionals and entrepreneurs.

EDITING

Suppose you are someone that has good writing and editing skills. In that case, proofreading and editing written documents is a great way for you to make some extra income. This is ideal for someone who may be in the field of writing and is looking to increase their writing skills while making money at the same time. There isn't a single platform dedicated to this type of work, but with a quick google search, you can find various freelance proofreading and editing gigs. You can usually make around $200 - $300 per written document depending on its length, so just proofreading a few documents per month can significantly increase your monthly income. Moreover, you can look into freelance writing, and there is growing popularity in hiring writers to write blogs, e-books, and articles.

If you want to make this into a passive income source as quickly as possible, you can find clients and hire other people to work as your writers or editors. This method will allow you to collect income without doing the actual grunt work.

FREELANCE WORK

When it comes to freelance work, there are a plethora of different types. You could do freelance work in whatever skill or profession you already have. For instance, you could do freelance work in writing music for productions or advertisements for musicians or do freelance music teaching. However, if you have other skills like writing or proofreading, you can pick up jobs online and make perfect money through numerous projects.

The benefit of freelance work is that you don't necessarily have to stick to one skill set. Using the numerous freelance work platforms available nowadays, such as Fiverr.com, Upwork.com, Freelancer.com, Peopleperhour.com, Writeraccess.com, and Freelancewriting.com, you can find side gigs that are suitable for your range of skills. When it comes to freelancing, you can pick up as many or as little gigs as you'd like and schedule them around your music. These websites above offer freelancers multiple different ways to make money. You could act as a ghostwriter and help people write books on topics you know about, or you could help a YouTube artist create background music without copyright for their channel, or you could simply help someone run a specific errand and get paid for it. The world is yours, and you can choose whatever suits your skills best. Below are a few examples of what freelance work encompasses.

- Fiverr.com

Fiverr.com is a platform that connects freelancers with specific skills to clients that require them. Most of the freelance skills on this website are more tech-related, including logo design, Word-Press, social media, SEO, and illustrations. If you have experience in design and technology (e.g., programming), then a lot of this work will be relevant to your skillset. They also offer different categories of skills, such as translation, data entry, book covers, and voice-overs. This platform could be a great way for you to build a freelance business.

- Upwork.com

Upwork.com is a platform that is similar to Fiverr that connects freelancers with specific skills to clients or agencies that require them. The categories that are included in Upwork are broader than Fiverr and include; Web, Mobile and Software development, Design & Creative, Writing, Sales & Marketing, Admin Support, Customer Service, Data Science and Analytics, and Engineering and Architecture. Some of these categories may require you to have the education and professional experience, but the categories such as Writing and Customer service may not. Any individual or agency can post freelance work gigs on Upwork.com to find the right person to fulfill their needs. This platform opens it up to big companies looking to hire someone for multiple projects that require the same skillset. Most of these gigs are done from home or online, so you can still maintain a flexible schedule and working environment, which will allow you to keep working on your music.

- Freelancer.com

Freelancer.com is similar to Upwork and Fiverr because it connects freelancers with specific skills to certain projects that require them. The most popular projects that freelancer.com receives include; website development, graphic design, Logo design, marketing, writing, and mobile app development. However, they have a huge selection of less popular categories but still have numerous projects posted daily. If you have any marketing experience or creating logos, you may find projects that require those skills and apply for them using this experience.

They also offer writing projects on this platform, so if you have experience writing articles, blogs, or e-books, this is the place to see what types of projects are available. Projects can range from $100 to over $500 + depending on the project size and skill type.

- Peopleperhour.com

Peopleperhour.com is similar to the above platforms as it connects freelancers to projects and businesses looking for a certain skill. The most popular projects on this platform include video shooting experts, Go developers, Children book illustrators, appointment setters, Swift developers, Visual merchandisers, Arabic translators, interior designers, music composers, and wealth managers. As you can see, music composer is a part of their most popular categories – this may be right up your alley.

Tons of businesses and individuals are looking for people who can compose songs they can use for their advertising or videos without copyright. It doesn't get taken down on popular platforms like YouTube. Moreover, if you have experience shooting videos at concerts or knowing any other languages, you could look into those projects as they are popular on this platform. For example, specific to music composing, freelancers on this website are charging anywhere from $30 - $100+ per hour to compose original music.

- Writeraccess.com

Writeraccess.com is different from the platforms that we just talked about as it is specific to writing, and you need to apply and get approved before you are matched with opportunities. If you are a strong writer and have experience writing blogs, books, articles, or e-books, then this is right up your alley. The books offered on this site are endless as they have writers who can write about agriculture to politics. Since you are a musician, you can specialize in the music industry in terms of writing, as you may have a strong knowledge of it already.

- Freelancewriting.com

Freelancewriting.com is a platform that matches freelance writers to specific companies and individuals that require their services. The freelance work offered on this platform includes; copywriting, content writing, project management, digital media management, SEO, RFP writing, and marketing. Writers can apply to these projects for free, while companies and individuals who seek these skills pay a fee to utilize their platform to find the right talent. These jobs are done from the comfort of your home so you can maintain your flexibility of hours and location.

INSTRUCTING: IN-PERSON LESSONS

This side hustle is also a very popular one and is so successful that many people have turned it into their main source of active income. Teaching lessons of some sort is a great business venture that can quickly turn into a source of passive income with the right approach.

- Personal Training

For example, if you are an ex-athlete or simply well-versed in the world of fitness, you can make anywhere from $40 - $100 per hour training other people in the gym. It is even better if you are someone in health and fitness and can also use this side hustle experience to boost your own resume and career. You can find clients in your city by posting ads, or you can provide virtual training using platforms like GymGo. Keep in mind that most people like to work out in the mornings or after work, so your main working hours would likely be before 9 am or after 5 pm. If you train for 10 hours a week, you can make anywhere from $400 - $1000 per week, leading to a monthly income of $1600 - $4000.

- Music Lessons

One example of course instruction that you can do with specific skills is teaching music lessons. If you are a musician or have strong music skills, this qualifies you to teach music lessons online or in your local music stores.

Teaching at local music stores or finding clients on your own can generate an income between $20 - $30+ per hour. This amount is a very good income compared to most side gigs and is in a field within your passion. Whether you find clients working at a music store or a teaching agency, you can host lessons in your home to increase flexibility. Running in-person music classes tends to make a bit more money than doing them online. Again, you must consider the flexibility factor as well. If you require a lot of flexibility, teaching music online is a better option but if you have an open schedule and a means of commuting to your students, then teaching in-person is a better option as you can make more money per hour.

When it comes to finding music teaching jobs in-person, do some research on your local music stores. Most music stores have a teaching department where they offer classes for a range of different instruments. You can simply walk in and introduce yourself with a resume and see if they have an opening, or you can go on their website and see if they have an application page. If you want to do this independently, you can put up an ad on your local buy/sell trade groups and offer your services. Finding your clients will generate the most income from all these options as you don't have to give a portion of it to the company that employed you. Moreover, you can choose to host your music lessons in your own home to increase flexibility.

Creating your own business will allow you to switch into passive income by hiring instructors to take over the business operations while making money as the owner.

INSTRUCTING: ONLINE COURSE INSTRUCTION

For example, if you are a musician, you can also look into music businesses looking to hire teachers. You can teach the instrument of your choice, and you don't have to work many hours, but you should be able to generate a decent income.

- Lessons.com

The largest and most popular platform for this type of work is lessons.com. Lessons.com is specialized in music teaching and offers teaching in sports, dance, health, fitness, martial arts, cooking, driving, painting, and many more. As a teacher, you can post your subject of expertise and have students sign up for your classes by paying a fee.

Lessons.com's earning potential varies a lot as it depends on how many people sign on to them. As a teacher, this platform allows you to contact potential students looking for specific lessons and send a quote for your services. Communication is mostly done online and is extremely flexible. However, its earning potential is lower than the other options we have explored earlier in the chapter.

INSTRUCTING: STARTING YOUR OWN BUSINESS

A great follow up to the two forms of income that we discussed above is a form of instruction where you create your own business. If you have specific skills such as music skills or fitness coaching skills, you can create your own business to instruct people in your specific skillset. This business can begin as an active source of income, where you coach people in your spare time, but can quickly become passive. You can turn this business into a source of passive income in no time. You can turn this into passive income by having a website or a subscription service set up. Once set up, people pay for your expertise or instruction in the form of email lists, online courses that you have pre-recorded, e-books that you have written, or any other form of instruction that you can pre-create and then sell to interested people.

This option can be challenging to get off the ground, as you need to find a following to generate business, but if you have it in you, this can be a great way to make passive income!

FINANCIAL INFORMATION

ALL MONEY MANAGERS or business owners are faced with risks; a lot of these risks are actually due to improper financial management and decision making. The decisions that you make for yourself and your business can make or break it. This chapter will be looking at how you can set yourself up for success as you begin this exciting but nerve-wracking endeavor.

WHAT IS FINANCIAL INTELLIGENCE?

Financial intelligence is something that everyone has deep inside of them; however, not many people know how to use it to its full potential. Some people have more awareness of financial intelligence and are naturally better at using their money to create more money.

The more you understand what financial intelligence is, the easier it will be to understand how to work with your money. In most cases, successful self-made people are always those with high financial intelligence. So, let's first define financial intelligence.

Financial intelligence is the ability to understand the various financial situations' ins and outs; this can vary from your company's finances, your employer's finances, or your finances. This chapter will learn how financial intelligence helps you and some characteristics of a financially intelligent person.

HOW TO DEVELOP FINANCIAL INTELLIGENCE

Being financially intelligent does not mean that you have to work yourself to the bone; it simply means that you need to have a certain set of skills to help you work smartly. These skills are generally in the form of self-discipline, mindset, and good habits. Let's look at how financial intelligence will help you and some financially intelligent people's characteristics.

- Financially intelligent people know money.

There is a big difference between what you know about money and what your beliefs are about money. Most people only understand the purchasing power that money brings, and that's about it. However, financially intelligent people know more than just that. They understand what their assets are and what their liabilities are. They understand the difference between a debit and a credit card, and usually, it's the lack of knowledge that causes people to make financial mistakes leading them to be in huge debt.

. . .

- Financial intelligence can help you increase your wealth.

Everybody wants to increase their wealth; that is a common fact. Those with high financial intelligence are simply more natural at doing it. Regardless of whether you are an entrepreneur or not, managing your money is important. People make a lot of money out of their existing money simply because they can control their cash flow at all times. You don't have to own a business to be financially intelligent; keeping track of your expenses, and managing that is enough to grow your financial intelligence.

- Financially intelligent people know what to do with their money.

Most people think that they aren't making enough money; although this is true in some cases, many people are not utilizing their money correctly. When you aren't utilizing your money correctly, people often believe that they are not making enough. The caveat to this is that the more money a person makes, the more inclined to spend they are. Financially intelligent people are not constantly chasing after more people; they typically find success by controlling their earnings. Typically, a financially intelligent person would aim to save at least 10% of their income, and they never touch it. That 10% is saved for investment purposes or kept as emergency money.

- Financially intelligent people have both short and long-term goals.

When it comes to money goals, financially intelligent people usually have a set of short term and long term goals. The ability to differentiate between these two types of goals will keep you balanced and focused. People typically forget about their long-term goals when faced with the simplicity of achieving their short term goals. To build future wealth, you MUST focus on your long term goals just as you focus on your short term goals. Typically, short term goals would be saving up for a 2-week vacation, while long-term goals would be saving up for a mortgage or business investment. If you spend the first $2,000 you save on a vacation, none of that money will ever touch your long-term goals. Financially intelligent people always make sure to achieve both without losing sight of either.

- Financial intelligence changes the way you relate to money.

As we mentioned earlier, your mindset is crucial to your entrepreneurial success. However, your mindset is also very important and has a large effect on your financial intelligence and success. Successful money people control their money, and they don't let their money control them. They decide where the money goes and doesn't allow money to determine where they go. Financially intelligent people are not afraid of money; they usually have complete control over all their finances.

FINANCIAL TERMS AND CONCEPTS YOU MUST KNOW

In this subchapter, I will be teaching you how to read and analyze your basic financial statements. These statements are usually; income statements, balance sheets, and cash flows. If you are someone who has gone to business school or taking finance/accounting at a college or university level, you probably already know this information. If not, you will want to pay extra attention. These concepts will apply to you even more once you start your own business or begin investing your money.

- Return On Investment (ROI)

Whether you are an investor or business owner, return on investment is an important analytical tool that you will need to use. The definition of ROI is; the ratio of a profit/loss made in a fiscal year expressed in terms of an investment.

This number is always expressed as a percentage increase or decrease related to the investment value during that fiscal year. Here is a simple example: if you invested $200 in stock and its value rises to $220 at the end of that fiscal year, your return on investment is 10%. In a more complicated example, if you invested $1000 in coffee bean stock for your coffee business and at the end of the year, you generated $2200 from selling coffee made by the beans (assuming no other costs or taxes are involved), your ROI is 220%.

Here is the formula for ROI: Net Profit/Total Investment x 100% = ROI

Let's use this formula in a different example.

Imagine that you are in the business of flipping houses. You purchased a cheap house during a courthouse auction for $75,000 and then spent $35,000 in materials for renovations. After the house's sale, commission, and expenses, you made $160,000 on the house. What would be your ROI?

First, you have to calculate your net profit- your total revenue subtracted from your total costs. In this case, that would be $160,000 – ($75,000 + $35,000), this gives you $50,000. Remember, your costs are purchasing the house ($75K) and the money you spend on materials ($35K).

Since ROI = Net Profit/Total Investment x 100

ROI = (50,000/110,000) x 100

ROI = 45 x 100

ROI = 45%

This simple equation may make house flipping sound easy but bear in mind that you can also lose money on an investment like this. If your investment is a loss, this formula will give you a negative number. Let's say, after everything, you could only sell the house for $90,000 as there are no other buyers. Take a look at the new ROI:

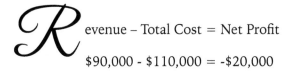

$\mathcal{R}$evenue – Total Cost = Net Profit

$90,000 - $110,000 = -$20,000

ROI = Net Profit/Total Investment x 100

ROI = (-20,000/110,000) x 100

ROI = -0.182 x 100

ROI = -18.2%

Essentially, you want your business to be yielding a positive number from your ROI; the higher, the better. If you yield a negative number, you may have to start rethinking your business plan or lower the business cost.

- Income Statements

An income statement is a bare minimum that you would need to know to manage your business's finances. An income statement's purpose is simple; it tells you whether you are profiting or losing money. Here is an example of a very simple income statement of a child's allowance:

Revenue or Gross Income: $5.00

Expenses: $2.00 (Candy)

Net income: $3.00

See how simple this is? The first line is the money coming into your possession. The second line is the money going out of your possession. The bottom line is the difference between the two. Since the number is positive, it means you are making money. If the net income is negative, it means you are losing money. Income statements can be as simple as such, but it does get more complicated the larger your company gets.

As companies grow larger and larger, they include a few more variations of the same structure. For instance, they may have additional lines such as; "cost of revenue" or "gross profit." They may also have additional lines differentiating their income, such as; "operating income" or "income before taxes." Entrepreneurs need to ensure that their income statements are accurate because they need to see whether their business is succeeding or not. An inaccurate income statement can cause you to think that your business is making more than it is (bad scenario) or making less than you think it is (better scenario).

- Fixed And Variable Costs

Now, let's learn about fixed and variable costs. The two main costs that a company has are variable costs and fixed costs. The variable cost differs based on the amount a business is producing, while the fixed costs remain the same regardless of how much output the business is producing. Let's take a look at variable cost first.

Variable Cost

A company's variable cost is directly related to the amount of goods/services it is producing. This cost will decrease or increase based on the production volume. When business production increases, the variable cost will rise. If the business product decreases, then the variable cost will decline. Variable costs will differ widely between various industries. Because of this, it is not useful for you to compare a coffee shop's variable costs to a car manufacturer because their product output is entirely different. It is better to compare the variable costs between two companies within the same industry, such as another coffee shop.

Variable costs are calculated by multiplying the quantity of output by the variable cost per unit of output. For instance, let's say company A produces ceramic plates for $2 per plate. If this company produces 500 units, the variable cost will be $1000. However, if the company has no orders and therefore does not produce any plates, then the variable cost would be $0. If the company gets a large order of 10,000 plates, the cost will rise to $20,000. This calculation does not take into account other costs, such as raw materials or labor.

Fixed Cost

A fixed cost is the other cost that any business or company will have. Different from the variable cost, the fixed cost does not change based on the volume of production. It will remain consistent even if no goods/services are produced. Therefore, this cost cannot be avoided.

Let's use the same example for company A. Imagine that Company A has a fixed cost of $10,000 per month to rent their plate producing machine. If the company has no orders for that month and doesn't produce any plates, they still have to pay $10,000 for the machine rental. However, let's imagine that they get a massive order of one million plates; the machine's rental remains the same; $10,000. However, the variable cost will be $2M in this example.

The higher the fixed cost is for a company, the more revenue they will require to break even. Therefore, the company will need to sell more products and work harder because these costs usually are unable to be lowered. The most common fixed costs examples are; building leases/rent payments, certain salaries, interest payments, insurance, and utilities.

Variable costs tend to remain consistent based on the number of goods the company produces, but the effects of fixed costs on a company's bottom line can differ based on the number of goods it produces. When production goes up, fixed cost decreases. The price of a larger amount of goods can be spread out over a fixed cost. Due to this, a company can achieve economies of scale.

For instance, if company A has a $10,000 monthly lease on its factory and it produces 1000 plates per month. It can spread the fixed cost of the lease at $10 per plate. ($10,000/1000 plates) However, if company A produces 10,000 plates per month, then its lease's fixed cost goes down to $1 per plate.

TIPS FOR HANDLING YOUR FINANCES

With all your new knowledge in financial intelligence, discipline training, goal setting, habit building, mindset development, and side gig/entrepreneur ideas, it is time to learn how to manage the extra money you'll save and make. In this section, I will be briefly walking you through what a good money manager looks like and the basics of money management.

Good money managers always share the same three characteristics. Firstly, they never spend beyond their means, ever. Even if there were a significant opportunity, they would never take out more money than they have to invest in it. Secondly, they always have a good stash of emergency savings. The emergency savings is where they have money saved up for a rainy day, so they don't have to go into debt or bankruptcy. Thirdly, good money managers assess their risks before taking one. This point does not mean they don't take any risks because you have to take risks as an entrepreneur. However, they take calculated risks. Let's cover the first characteristic first.

- Good Money Managers Will Never Spend Beyond Their Means

Good money managers will never spend more than they already have. What does this mean? It means that they will never spend more money than they have in their immediate accounts. Most good money managers will have some savings reserved for emergency purposes. That stash of money does not get touched unless it is for emergencies. They also will never take out a loan or pay for things with a credit card if they don't already have that existing money in their debit accounts. Not spending beyond your means will prevent you from getting yourself into debt.

Moreover, most people that spend beyond their means usually spend their money on non-essential things. They may be tempted to buy a new car as a big sale at a local dealership is temping them due to low monthly rates. Good money managers will not spend their money on a new car unless it is utterly essential for their living. Further, they will not spend money on this unless they are 100% sure they can pay off the car without needing to sign up for ridiculously high-interest rates or long financing terms.

- Good Money Managers Always Have Emergency Savings

Emergencies happen to everyone. It can come in the form of a flooded basement or a large medical bill. Good money managers are people that avoid living paycheck to paycheck. Instead, they make an effort to save at least 10% of their income every month into their emergency savings. The purpose of emergency savings is to prevent unforeseen circumstances from bankrupting you. Those who live paycheck to paycheck without any sort of emergency savings can be thrown into financial turmoil if they are suddenly stuck with a $5,000 medical bill. As a rule of thumb, aim to have $10,000 of emergency savings that you can dip into if an expensive accident happens. This emergency fund will prevent you from needing to stress or needing to take out a high-interest loan to pay for the emergency.

- Good Money Managers Take Calculated Risks

Good money managers only take calculated risks. You often hear of people purchasing and selling stocks to make a lot of money quickly. Although this does work, there is a ton of risk involved. Good money managers usually would not take risks such as purchasing stock as there is no guaranteed return. Instead, they usually use their money to invest in other financial products that have less risk. For instance, a common investment that good money managers like to invest in is real estate. Although you require quite an initial hefty sum of money, its return is usually quite high. Here is an example. Kate has savings of $30,000 and is looking for an investment. She is deciding between investing her $30,000 into several different types of stocks or using her $30,000 as a down payment for a house. If Kate were a good money manager, the choice she would make would be to invest $30,000 in a house as long as the real estate in her market is steady. Usually, house prices increase by 5% - 10% every year, which guarantees her an investment return of 5% - 10%. If she chooses to invest her $30,000 into stocks, she is putting her money at a lot of risks as stocks can drop in price in a matter of days while the housing market typically takes longer to drop, and you are provided with much more notice. By simply looking at these two options, a good money manager will see that investing in real-estate is the safer choice with high returns. If you are just starting to manage your money, don't dabble with stocks unless you have knowledge and experience first.

HOW TO SET YOURSELF UP FOR FINANCIAL SUCCESS

All money managers or business owners are faced with risks; a lot of these risks are actually due to improper financial management and decision making. The decisions that you make for yourself and/or your business can make or break it. This section will look at how to set yourself up for financial success as you begin building your passive income business.

Track Revenue Per Hour

When starting a business, it is essential to track how much time you spend on it. You must track this to determine your revenue and profits per hour. Let's say you needed 10 hours of work to jumpstart your business (e.g., getting a website/social media built, advertising, business development), and you managed to get yourself your first two clients. We are going to use the example of a coaching business to illustrate this concept.

Since coaching sessions are usually one hour in length and may happen 1 – 3 times a week, you need to divide your profit by how many total hours you've put into it. For example, let's pretend that your two existing clients agree to three coaching sessions per week for an open-ended amount of time. They may only need one month of coaching in total, or they may require several years, but they are playing that by ear. Here are the numbers for this example:

10 hours (setting up the business)

2 Existing Clients (3 sessions per week)

$150 per session (1 hour)

In your first week of coaching your clients, the above points demonstrate that you have made ($150 x 3 sessions x 2 clients) $900. This amount sounds like a lot, but if you divide it out by the amount of time you put in, your revenue per hour is only $56 per hour. Of course, you have to keep in mind that the initial 10 hours that you've put into your business at the beginning is a one-time occurrence. Still, you have to factor in the hours OUTSIDE of the sessions where you are scheduling, managing, and developing your business.

In other words, what I'm saying is that you must do these calculations before dedicating a generous amount of time to your business. If there are other side hustles out there that don't require such a large amount of time and pay more than $56 per hour, you may want to consider those options too. Be sure to look into all of these options before settling on a side hustle.

Reduce Expenses

Now, let's look at a few strategies and tips that your company can use to reduce its expenses. There are only two ways to increase your business profits; you could either increase your sales or reduce your expenses. Increasing sales is typically the harder route as it will involve a lot of strategies, planning, and moving pieces to pull off. However, reducing business expenses is something that is much easier to do and takes less time. Let's take a look at a few different ways that you can reduce business expenses to generate a larger bottom line.

1. Go digital

Printing costs are a huge expense that most companies don't realize can add up very quickly. The cost of ink, paper, and machine maintenance costs a small fortune, and a lot of time is wasted dealing with silly printing issues. As an entrepreneur, try to eliminate paper usage as much as possible to cut costs and streamline your business. Go digital as much as possible and take advantage of free software like Google drive and online signature services. This method will also prevent problems like misplaced documents. Having everything digital will allow you and all of your employees to access important information quickly and cheaply.

2. Buy from big service providers

Big service providers typically have the lowest prices for materials you require, as they can operate on a lower profit margin. Smaller local options may seem better at first glance as they can customize their offerings to meet your needs. However, do some research on the big service providers first to see if they have any customizable offerings. This simple solution can help reduce your operating costs significantly.

3. Insurance

Depending on what your company offers, you may need to invest in some insurance. This insurance could include liability insurance, building insurance, or car insurance. You need to regularly review your agreement with your insurance provider to determine if another company can offer you a better deal. It doesn't take much time to do this, and it can easily save you thousands of dollars every year while your company is still receiving the same benefits. Some start-up insurance companies offer cheaper insurance premiums as they have lower costs by taking away office spaces and offering fully-remote work to their employees.

4. Hiring freelancers instead of staff when possible

Assess your company's needs when you feel like you require new talent to fix a business problem or improve your business. If you require a website makeover, you don't need to hire a full-time web developer to do this job. You can hire a freelancer easily to do the same job but without the long-term commitment. Outsource your work to contractors or freelancers whenever you can, but don't cheap out on them. Good contractors and freelancers typically cost a little bit more, but it's much better to pay more upfront for high-quality work than to have to pay someone else to fix it later.

5. New equipment does not perform that much better than used equipment

It is nice to buy new items but ensure that you assess the value of the new item you are buying compared to a similar second-hand item. For instance, if you start up a coffee shop, look around your neighborhood buy and sell websites and forums to see if you can find the espresso machine model that you want but second hand. Most of the time, good equipment remains in good health even after many years, so buying a new espresso machine may not give you any additional benefits. Buying a second-hand machine may cost much less and provide you with the same services that you require.

6. Don't spend money on needless office space

If you do not regularly have clients coming and going, move your office space to somewhere less expensive or get rid of it altogether. With our convenient technology nowadays, you can even offer your employees remote work to reduce the amount of physical space you need. If you require weekly meetings with your employees, rent a one-time space, or make it fun by having it at a local restaurant or bar.

LEGAL INFORMATION YOU SHOULD KNOW BEFORE STARTING A BUSINESS

At this point in the book, we want to wrap up everything you have learned. I kept this chapter until the end as it is less focused on the directions and strategies for choosing and starting a passive income business but is more so focused on tying up any loose ends. Although this part of starting up your side hustle may seem boring, it is extremely crucial as not doing some of these steps can lead to legal trouble down the road. We all know how time-consuming and expensive that is, so let's avoid this by being prepared.

Here are a few items you need to prepare for depending on what kind of passive income source you have chosen and what location you will be running your new business (if this is what you have chosen).

- Is your business name legal?

Before you start building your side hustle business website and begin its marketing, make sure that another business doesn't already purchase the name you have chosen. Depending on what country you live in, there should be a free online search where you can look up all registered business names. It will then tell you whether your business name has already been taken in your residence area. Make sure to do this step before you invest any money into the business name you've come up with.

- Register a DBA or Fictitious Business Name

If your side hustle business uses a different name from your legal name, then you must register for a DBA (doing business as) to use for filing for all paperwork purposes. For example, your name is Mike Smith, and your business name is "Beautiful Properties." This requirement is normal practice for businesses in the U.S. but may vary from country to country. Make sure you look into your country's requirements and have it completed to avoid any government penalties.

- Incorporate Your Business & Get A Tax ID

Incorporating your business may vary for you, depending on which country you are from. This requirement is important for all tax purposes, and different business structures have different ways of filing/doing taxes. If you don't do this, you will likely operate your business illegally and face numerous fines. Once you decide which business structure you want to go with for your side hustle business, you need to register for a tax I.D. number. This number will function as your business's identification with the government. This number will allow the government to audit/track your business transactions. Failure to do this may lead to fines and jail time for evading taxes.

- Educate Yourself On Employee Laws

Depending on whether you want to grow your side hustle business into a firm or not, you must educate yourself on employment laws. If you hire someone to work for your business, you must understand your obligations for taxes, payroll, unemployment insurance, wage & hour requirements, workers' compensation, and anti-discrimination laws. Moreover, you can also hire contractors to avoid some of these liabilities, but you would need to educate yourself on those laws. Make sure you get a good understanding before bringing someone else on board to avoid any lawsuits.

- Obtain the Necessary Business Permits and Licenses

Depending on where you live globally, your side hustle business may require you to get a permit or a license before it can legally operate. There are many different types of coaching licenses – make sure you educate yourself on which one you need depending on your specialization and your country of residence. You should also look into whether you need a special permit to run your side hustle business. Most countries do not require this, but it's better to be safe than to have your business shut down for illegal practices.

- File For Trademark Protection

Although you are not legally required to trademark your business, you can avoid future headaches by trademarking your business name to avoid anybody using your brand for their benefit. This filing may not be necessary if you are just starting your side hustle business, but as it becomes more successful and well-known, this is a step that you should remember to do to protect yourself and your business.

- Open A Business Bank Account

Opening a business bank account for your side hustle business will not only help you separate your personal finances from your business ones, but it will also help you build business credit so you can take out loans in the future as needed. Go to your local bank and find the best business banking account deal and make use of their offerings. They usually can offer a business banking account with deals or business credit cards that help you collect points.

HOW TO MAKE THIS A REALITY

Now that you are equipped with all of the technical knowledge that you need to find or create the perfect source of passive income for you, we will spend this chapter learning some tips and tricks that will help you find the most success possible. Keep these tips in mind as you begin pursuing your passive income source, especially when you face challenges along the way.

HOW TO GET STARTED

Goal setting is the first action that a person needs to take to reach their goals. The purpose of setting a goal is so that a person can achieve their desired results. When a goal is set carefully with focus, momentum, action, and intention, setting and achieving goals is the first step a person needs to take to move from where they are not to where they want to be. However, they need to know where they want to be—the "where" begins with a person envisioning it.

CHALLENGES YOU MAY FACE

As you begin your journey to creating your side hustle, it is important to recognize that you will likely face some obstacles. By accepting this fact before they arise, you will not be surprised, but rather you will feel prepared.

Before you begin, take some time to write in your journal about what some possible obstacles may be. Once you have done this, take some time to plan and decide how you will deal with them when they arise so that they do not disrupt your progress or cause you to resort to old ways that are unhealthy.

By setting yourself up for success in this way, you will be able to tackle any challenge without having your new lifestyle jeopardized.

Although your business will require you to spend time working on the administrative tasks and streamlining the infrastructure, you should not spend all your time there. What you need to focus on is generating business by either selling or working. Spend most of your working hours for your coaching business to market and sell your products and services and deliver them. All successful entrepreneurs spend more time working FOR their business rather than IN their business.

THE RIGHT MINDSET FOR SUCCESS

Mindset is crucial when it comes to financial intelligence. The way you think and feel about money has everything to do with how you spend it and save it. People with negative mindsets towards money such as; "I never have enough of it anyway, might as well buy this new television now" or "If I don't spend it on something I like, the money will go elsewhere." Mindsets like this cause your finances to always get you stuck in a vicious cycle. Financially intelligent people typically have strong self-discipline. In many cases, self-discipline is the key to financial success.

Many researchers suggest that the single most important thing in a person's ability to become financially successful is their self-discipline level. Self-discipline is responsible for helping people stay focused on reaching their goals, giving them the grit that they need to stick with difficult tasks, and overcoming barriers and discomforts as they push themselves to achieve greater things. Let's refresh our memory on the definition of self-discipline. Self-discipline is the ability of a person to control their impulses, reactions, behaviors, and emotions. It allows them to let go of instant gratification in exchange for long-term gain and satisfaction. It's the act of saying no when you want to say yes. Self-discipline isn't about living a restrictive and boring life without any enjoyment. It's almost impossible to be 100% self-disciplined in every single area of your life. Rather than trying to be disciplined at everything you do, you can use it to focus on the most important things.

HOW TO BUILD HEALTHY HABITS TO FIND SUCCESS

- People cannot achieve their financial goals without using self-discipline.

People cannot achieve their financial goals without self-discipline, so make sure you supplement your goals with a self-discipline list. It will help you focus on the tasks and behaviors you need to perform to achieve your goals. For example, one of your goals is to save $2,000 in 6 months. Your discipline list will include putting aside at least $350 every month and avoiding spending money on unnecessary things like fancy restaurants or video games. High self-discipline in this example would be doing everything on that list without any exception. It does not mean that you cannot reward yourself or take a break from working towards your goals; it simply means that you should get the things done on your list before indulging in any rewards.

- Use a daily list to track your finances and to monitor unnecessary spending.

Make sure you are using a daily list to keep track of all the things you need to get done to achieve your goals. Try to use online tools or just a simple notebook that can help you prioritize and organize. It feels very satisfying to check off items that you've completed, and it will even motivate you to finish other tasks that are on your list just to feel the satisfaction of being able to check off another box. Make sure your to-do list works hand-in-hand with your discipline list to help yourself stay on track. A useful tip to keep in mind when you're feeling unmotivated is to start with the easiest item on the list just to get the ball rolling. Once you complete one easy task, people normally feel more motivated than before; this will help you get started on the rest of your list. Starting with a harder task may create apprehension about doing it; therefore, start small and work your way up.

- Figure out which obstacles are holding you back from success.

Different people have different things that distract them from being able to complete important tasks. For example, a person that is easily distracted by emails and people in their office might have to close their office door as soon as they get into work to get their tasks done. They may delay any phone calls or meetings unless they're necessary for completing their set of responsibilities. This method is effective for people that may be trying to lose weight. For example, if they know that junk food is their weakness, instead of resisting eating junk food in their house, they can simply eliminate all the junk food in their house, so they don't have access to it. You must minimize and remove all temptations of the distractions that affect you the most when reaching your most important goals.

- Share your financial goals with other people.

It may be easier for some people to stick with completing a goal when they have made a public commitment. The thought of failing to reach a goal in front of other people can motivate them to stick with it. You can also take this one step further and ask those people to hold you accountable as well. If you aren't sharing your goals with anyone, nobody will know if you have been slacking off from it. When nobody is there to hold you accountable, you will likely be less motivated to keep doing it since nobody will know if you failed.

- Use external sources or motivation as well as internal.

A saying goes, "don't do it for others; do it for yourself." However, some people find that they are much more disciplined when they know that their impulses, emotions, behaviors, and actions affect other people. Contrary to popular belief, it's alright to use external sources to help your motivation. Sometimes, motivation coming from external sources is more powerful than internal motivation. Find the purpose beyond yourself that is important to you to help give you a higher chance of success.

- Discipline is created by creating habits.

When something becomes a habit, you no longer need to draw from your will power bank to get yourself to do it. For example, if your goal was to stop spending money at restaurants for lunch during the workday, get into the habit of making yourself fulfilling meals to prevent yourself from buying food when you're at the office. You will be able to see the benefits of saving money if you can stick with it. Once you see the benefit, you will have more motivation to keep doing it, and soon it becomes a habit where it will feel strange not to make your meals. This way, you will no longer need to draw from your bank of self-control, but instead, meal-prepping will come naturally since it has become a habit of yours.

- Stop making excuses.

Don't procrastinate, or wait for tomorrow, do it now. If you fall off the wagon, that's okay. Start over immediately. Stop telling yourself that something is too hard, or there's something that you cannot change. Don't blame other people for the circumstances that you're in. Making excuses is the Kryptonite of self-discipline. Achieve a mindset that is more about "I can do this" rather than "I'll do it tomorrow."

AFTERWORD

Congratulations, and thank you for reaching the end of this book! You have successfully taken the first step towards beginning a side hustle and developing a second income source for yourself.

First things first, pat yourself on the back for reading until the end of this book! You have taken the first important step in building your source of passive income. You should now have a solid knowledge of how to jumpstart your side hustle or create a business and manage it as it grows into a source of passive income.

TIPS AND TRICKS

Throughout this book, you have been given numerous ideas for making money utilizing side gigs, which can eventually become a passive income source for you.

For example, if you are really enjoying teaching music lessons online, but you're only averaging about $10 per hour, you may want to try out a different side gig or another way to deliver the music lessons that could earn you more money. Never stay stuck on one side gig if it's not working out for you.

You should also consider learning hard skills that pay well, such as contracting or maintenance work, as you can pick up projects that pay well whenever you like.

When you figure out what the most desired skills are where you live and what type of work is in the highest demand, you can improve your skills and cater to those needs. Finding this out will help you generate the most income while pursuing a passive income business.

Another tip is to schedule hours specifically for you to work on your business. This step is crucial for your success. When your regular workday ends, your business working hours are starting. Schedule off blocks of time during those hours and stick to it. Doing this will prevent you from giving up quickly because you're 'not seeing progress' if you are consistently putting in the work to start your business.

I want to leave you with one final piece of advice before you venture off on your own. A critical takeaway from this book is to make sure you are trying different kinds of side gigs depending on how much money you're making and your level of enjoyment. There must be a balance between both.

Lightning Source UK Ltd.
Milton Keynes UK
UKHW020921311220
376198UK00013B/1036

9 781087 936642